Shattered Glass

Mike Gouchie

Copyright 2025 by Mike Gouchie
Editors JL Cartwright, JD Shipton
Cover artist Michelle Lee

All rights reserved. Without limiting the rights under copyright reserved above, no part of this publication may be reproduced, stored in or introduced into a retrieval system, or transmitted, in any form, or by any means (electronic, mechanical, photocopying, recording, or otherwise) without the prior written permission of both the copyright owner and the publisher of this book.

Digital ISBNs
EPUB 9780228635659
Kindle 9780228635666
Coresource 9780228635673
PDF 9780228635680

Print ISBNs
Amazon print 9780228635697
Ingram Spark 9780228635703
Barnes and Noble 9780228635635
BWL Print 9780228635642

Dedication

A dedication to those who fell short on fame, yet remain large at heart

Acknowledgement

BWL Publishing acknowledges the Government of Canada and the Canada Book Fund for its financial support in creating the Canadian Historical Mysteries collection.

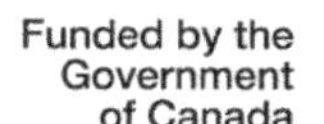

BWL Publishing acknowledges the Province of Alberta for their ongoing support through the Alberta Publisher's Cultural Industry Operating Grant.

Table of Contents

Prologue

Whether on a sundeck, in a living room, a pub, a plane, or a boat. Someone tells a story about meeting someone famous, or maybe their own hit and miss chances with success. Anyone who's ever dabbled in the music Business (small m Capital B), has a story and/or a history with their own level of fame. "This one's mine…"

If I had a dime for every time someone said,

Why didn't you make it? I'd probably have enough for a burger and fries (ok, maybe just fries…)

Most annoying, *you should've never given up on music.* So, I guess this is a good opportunity to say, "I've never given up on music."

Sure, for reasons often beyond my reach or control, life has just gotten in the way. Can't say *I was forced* to become a realist, because I was given opportunities to make good or bad decisions.

And often as they say, *the struggle was real.*

Sometimes an artist wants something so bad, they'll sacrifice everything the *Music Industry* imposes on them, to get *it.*

Things such as (but, not always) relationships, family, friends, secure careers, and definitely – *and far too often* -- money you don't have.

Oh, and one other small detail, *selling your soul,* cause, once selfishness is achieved (especially when nearly achieved), many prefer to get back what they had…

Chapter 1

Devil Lurking

I was a quiet kid. Usually did chores before anyone asked and was always close to my mother's side. Don't remember a lot from my childhood. But musically, here's what happened…

The earliest memory of anything musical in my life started after a traumatizing childhood event that is still indescribable, even after many decades of reflecting thoughts and inner personal dialogue. There is no real answer as to what happened and why, only personal speculation.

The Devil came in the night and lingered by my dimly lit bedroom door. He came walking by and peering in, lunging past (ghostlike) back and forth, as if to tell me, *you're my next victim.* I was being stalked, and I knew for sure; he was there to violently rip out my soul.

I hid beneath the covers frozen in fear, unable to move, unable to speak. I'd open my mouth to yell for help, but nothing would come out. I was truly terrified.

There was absolute total silence, at least I have no memory of there being any sound whatsoever.

My bed was a cold block of ice slowly turning into a bubbling pit of black lava. My mind was racing as screams came from deep within telling me to escape before it was too late. *"You can do it, you can do it, you can do it…"*

With the hovering demon still lurking in the distance I gathered every ounce of courage I had, and slowly and methodically pulled down my cover, which felt like a sheet of metal shackling me to my tiny mattress.

Slowly the top of my head pops out, then the sheet slides down to the bottom of my eyes. I take a short peek, but only for a moment, then when I see nothing, I wonder. *Is he gone? Or, is he just waiting on the other side of the door?*

I remember the doorway being lit by a distant light, maybe from the bathroom or the hood over the kitchen stove.

The bedroom and hallway were carpeted, so if I was going to make a run for it, at least I'd have some traction. After all, my parents room was probably less than 12 feet away. All I had to do was squiggle slowly and silently out of my bed, bolt for the door across the hall, turn the handle, open the door, run like crazy and jump into their bed.

Had the devil lost interest in me, or was he just lying in wait?

I gathered every ounce of courage and slid strategically out of the tight sheet and covers. I opened my eyes just long enough to get my bearings, then I ran, first on tip toes and then in a full out sprint. My eyes opened ever so briefly, just to see and grab the doorknob, turn it, and fling it open. Finally with one last lunge, I reached safety.

I never said a word. I just wiggled in and fell asleep. As far as my parents knew, one of their kids climbed in and crashed for the night...

Of course there's thoughts of, *was it just my young imagination*? Not a chance.

Because what happened soon afterwards put it all into perspective.

I still don't recall any tears, just a vivid feeling of terror, streaking from my cold dark room to my parent's room where I sank down into peace and comfort.

The following night, as I fought with my scared of the dark demons, I closed my eyes and fell asleep (probably with a light on).

Suddenly a sound in the night startled me awake, *huh, what's that...?*

An indescribable feeling came over me. It was eerie yet comforting. And an angelic voice soothed me with a heavenly sound. Slowly I faded into a hypnotic state of comfort. With an unworldly sound playing in the background of my mind, a wordless voice spoke to me and said, *you are safe.* The voice told me I had no reason to be afraid and

that everything was going to be okay.

Without anyone physically wrapping their arms around me, a warm and comforting embrace flowed over me and throughout my entire body.

It still resonates in the back of my mind to this day. No name, no voice, nor worldly sound has ever compared.

That speechless voice of comfort had no outer volume, it had no flat or high tone. It was not male or female, nor young nor old... yet, it still has the ability to reach the depths of my soul.

I know it sounds odd (even to me), but growing up this invisible sound was my closest friend, and later on in life, it became the most reliable. It was my *protector,* and I believe it to be the reason I've survived so many near misses, throughout my life...

I call this sound/noise/voice, *my inner music.*

Unfortunately, I forced that voice to sleep far too many times over the years.

I admit, I took the voice for granted most of my life. I only used it when I was down and out and really needed someone (or something) to dig me out of my deepest darkest holes.

There were times I would try to wake that voice, but I never stuck it out, and in moments of weakness I'd just give up when things became too difficult.

It's funny how that *other* voice is not worth mentioning and too often not worth acknowledging becomes so much louder at times?

Anyways...

The good voice was always welcoming and would awaken, when I became desperate and sobbing pitifully and feeling sorry for myself.

Once again on my last dime, sloppy crying, deep in prayer trying to waken it, "*please, please, help me*". Down and out on my last breaths that's when my *inner music* would awaken, and oddly enough for some selfish crazy reason that's just what it would take to get me to finally listen. And then, when I listened, good things would happen. Makes sense right?

So why, one wonders, didn't I follow that voice every day and live a happy life. I'm sure that's a question we all ask ourselves from time to time. I guess for me, most times when it answered, I just didn't like what it had to say. So, I'd let the louder voice win with whatever stupidity or nonsense it had to spew at the time.

Usually things like, *Follow me, trust me, I'll help you get where you need to be.*

As an adult, *The Devil Lurking* would reach out from around that corner, grab me and pull me in.

I took my *inner music* voice seriously, but unfortunately, I never learned how to truly accept that voice until much later in life.

It wasn't until I could truly stop, listen, and finally accept the voice's reasoning, that better opportunities came to fruition in my life.

I always believed there was something more for me, but I never surrounded myself with the ones who could support getting me there until later in life, when I'd learned that sometimes you have to get there on your own.

Chapter 2

Part 1: Music Roots

I come from a deep background of family musicians and singers. My father would say, "Everyone in the family is a singer, even the sewing machine".

On one side of the family a concert pianist worthy grandfather, with several multi-instrumentalist children and a grandmother driving us through the backroads singing a 1960 song "The Squaws Along The Yukon" (now deemed inappropriate). She'd sing away "Ooga Looga Looshka, which means that I love you, If you'll be my baby I'll Ooga Looga Looshka you".

Unbeknownst to Granny D, Ma tells a story of how she used to bring kids home from school, charge them 10 cents each and they'd sneak under the cabin's kitchen window and listen to Gramma sing.

On Pops side, there's flashbacks of Grandpa on a harmonica, Pops on guitar strumming and singing with folks dancin', jiggin', and shaking up the floor.

My early days as a kid were steeped in traditional country and the bare roots of Rock and Roll. I'm talking Hank Snow, Buck Owens, Johnny Cash, Merle Haggard and yes, The Possum himself Mr. George Jones.

This led into the Elvis era, with Buddy Holly, Ritchie Valens, Chuck Berry, and The Beatles.

Later came the richness of gospel tones...

There was music playing at all times. When my father wasn't working, he had a band and played the community halls for social events, dances, and weddings. And, if there wasn't a gig, there was always a party at our place.

From what I'm told, there was as much drinking and fighting back in those days, as there was playing and singing. And, apparently there was a lot of both.

At around 6 years old I learned the New Seekers 1971 song "Never Ending Song of Love" for a local talent contest, which was held in Vaniah Hall in Prince George. It was a big deal. My father played guitar while I sang. I belted out the song and earned a third place finish.

My brother Buddy placed first and Gary Fjellgaard landed second. Gary went on to become a well-known name in Canadian Country music.

After that, pretty much all I remembered was my father and brother playing music together. Don't believe I ever lost interest, just never received the attention of first place.

Part 2: The Music Changed

When I was about seven years old: My father, "drunk" on Christmas Eve, walked my blind Great Grandmother across the frozen Fraser River.

From the sawmill side of the Shelley (Lheidli T'enneh) Indian reservation to the other side, where an old Catholic Church still stands. This is where my parents were married, and my granny would attend midnight mass once a year.

As they walked the aisle of the church preparing for midnight mass, my father fell to his knees...

Alongside my granny, and in the presence of God, he asked for forgiveness for the life he had led to that point.

Overnight, the music changed.

Gospel became the new voice and sound that lit the house, replacing anything and everything else with a beat. It was joyful and uplifting. Everyone seemed happy.

"I'd like to think my mother secretly tucked away all her favorites for rainy days". Then, when pops wasn't around to scorn her for giving into the flesh, she'd listen to the county classics...

My father re-wrote all his favorite country songs, and turned them into gospel versions, so that being gospel, he could feed his cravings and sing without guilt.

There was no more room in our home, car, or any family gathering for the devil's music. Religion became an obsession for my pops.

My father had a tough upbringing, which led to residential school, then fighting like hell to become an adult. He worked hard but had no real direction, other than partying, playing music and fighting. All that changed when he found the Bible, and the Holy Spirit filled him with the unconditional love he had missed as a child.

When he spoke of God, he beamed from ear to ear, and I believed he could recite every scripture from memory. Even when the bible was closed and grasped tightly in his hand, he'd recite every word correctly, then he'd tell you the chapter and verse, and he always had it right.

I remember an American preacher friend of my dad's taking our family on a trip to some Northern BC communities.

Along the way we stop at a roadside pull out, where another kid and I take the opportunity to burn off some energy. We run down a steep path below the pullout towards, Telegraph Creek. The other kid was a few steps ahead of me and steps on a yellow jackets' nest. My forward momentum lunges me directly into the massive swarm! They relentlessly continue to sting me as I made my way down the rest of the hill and jump into the shallow "knee high" stream. We were far away from any medical treatment, but the American preacher and my father laid hands on me for healing. Within minutes the stingers fell out, and I was up running around and playing.

Although our home was now strictly religious, music still played an important role. The drinking and partying was replaced by loud joyous music and nightly prayer meetings.

Those nights there were always a lot of people in the house. They'd be celebrating and singing to the lord, with some of them speaking in tongues and calling on miracles. There was always someone being saved.

Some nights the prayer meetings would run quite late, but it was okay, because it was God provoked. Ma would let it go on for a little while, but then she'd step in and shut things down, so we could get some sleep. Especially if it was a school night.

The religious Nazi era ended when I was in my teens. Pops became more spiritual, rather than religious.

He was a beautiful man who was always filled with an abundance of love. Everyone was accepted for whoever they were, no matter their circumstances. Dad often brought someone who was down and out, home with him. Ma would make sure they were fed and clothed warmly.

It was especially normal around Christmas, to have a visitor. Dad would bring out his guitar, sing some gospel songs and tell them about his journey to a better life. My father made many, many lifelong friends.

Our last Christmas (two months prior to his passing) together, my Pops pulled me aside for a heart to heart. He told me, "Mike, you are the closest thing I ever had to a father".

Such a powerful statement and something I've reflected on time and time again. Realizing the tough life he had growing up (without direction) and what an amazing father he had become himself. That only multiplied even further, with the love for his grandchildren.

I feel his spirit often and am comforted knowing he's sheltered in the arms of his heavenly father.

Chapter 3

School Days

The middle school years were filled with gospel music at home and church. And of course, school Christmas concerts.

One year's Christmas concert, we sang about reindeer racing through the sky in the blazing sun.

The next year, our teacher sent us home with a can of shoe polish, and had our parents paint our faces, hands, and arms black for the concert.

Then our dads drilled holes in long 2x4's and brought them in to line the front of stage. On concert night the holes were stuffed with willow branches, and their twigs were covered with cotton balls.

Showtime.

My brother Buddy was in Grade 7, and he played guitar for my Grade 5 class. I can still see the picture of that stage filled with around 20 kids, all painted black, and wearing an assortment of straw hats and old clothing.

The music started:

"Jump down turn around pick a bale of cotton, jump down turn around pick a bale a day. Oh Lordy, pick a bale of cotton. Oh Lordy, pick a bale a day".

We all squatted down after each verse, grabbed handfuls of cotton balls off the twigs, and stuffed them into bags the teacher had us hang around our necks.

What did that have to do with Christmas? And, why did a bunch of kids have to be painted up black and sing a song about picking cotton, for a Christmas concert? I never did figure that one out? I was more athletic than anything else in my early teen years. I was never great academically, but I did win a mathematician award before I moved on to focus on sports.

In Grade 7 I was awarded Athlete of the Year, and again in Grade 10.

In grade 10, I also signed up for band class and as the drummer learned once again, how to count to four.

On a band trip ferry from Prince Rupert to Port Hardy, a bottle of home made wine found it's way into my roomies luggage (I swear it was his luggage). But, when we opened the bottle in our room it exploded and made a huge mess.

There was wine covering the ceiling and walls of our tiny cabin. We found towels in the bedding closet and managed to clean it all up and stash the evidence before our chaperone (Mr. B) came by to check on us.

Mr. B walked in and said, "it smells bad in here boys." He turned on a fan above the doorway and in minutes the smell was gone...

High school talent night "The Gong Show". Ron and Aaron on guitar, Debbie on bass and vocals, Karen on vocals and myself on drums. We played our version of "Crimson and Clover" and won first place.

During high school I started writing songs and singing. This only happened in private.

No one knew that I wrote songs and sang to myself all the time.

I remember learning Kris Kristofferson's "The Pilgrim" alone in my room. I sang that song quietly to myself over and over and over, until I memorized ever word. I don't believe anyone ever heard me singing. Oddly enough, I've never sung the song since that time.

The first song I recall writing, was a love song called "Lovin' You". It actually ended up on my first ever professionally recorded EP titled "One of a kind".

I'd sing privately to girls, pretending to be someone famous. It usually went over well...

Chapter 4

The Next Chapter

My teenage years were filled with sports. I was heavy into boxing, kickboxing, and bodybuilding.

Girls controlled my thoughts throughout my early years. And, if I'm being honest, most of the years that followed...

I moved away from my hometown for work when I was 19. At that time Karaoke was becoming a *thing*, so I hooked up with a girl from my hometown, and we started singing at the local pubs and bars.

I think that's when I became most comfortable singing. A different town where no one knew me, and I could just sing...

Soon it seemed as though a microphone was glued to my hand. It was meant to be.

I entered my first Karaoke contest while in Kamloops, and I won first place. It was a trip for two to Mexico, or the cash equivalent. I took the cash.

Songs: *Kenny Rogers* "She Believes In Me" and *Ben E King* " Stand By Me" were my go to's.

During that time, I recorded a couple vocal tracks to minus mixes (music with no vocals) like *Clint Black* and *Vince Gill* at a local studio.

Hell, I may still even have one or two of those old cassettes kicking around the basement somewhere?

A local girl was looking for a male vocal on a project she was doing, so I did my best to accompany her on "Wind Beneath My Wings". I see her on social media from time to time, still kicking out singles to radio with her band.

I worked full time in the maintenance department at Stockman's Hotel while living in Kamloops and picked up extra shifts with any other department that needed help as well.

At the year end Christmas party, they had a picture of me with the caption, "I'll do anything, but wash toilets with my hair". It was true and got some laughs.

One day after work, I walked into a Chinese restaurant to grab some take-out, to bring back to my rented room on St. Paul St. close to Stockman's.

There was a girl in the restaurant with a couple guys I knew from back home in Prince George and she gave me her number. A week or so later I found the number when emptying my pockets to do laundry. I called her and we started dating. Her dad was a part of the Army Navy Club and a big Dwight Yoakam fan.

He loved it when I'd show up to the Sunday Jams sessions and sing Dwight's, "Guitars & Cadillacs, Honky Tonk Man, Long white Cadillac and Little Sister".

I made it a regular thing, and was getting quite comfortable on stage with a band.

In the meantime, I'd heard some old high school friends were planning of putting a country rock touring band together. Word had it, they had a couple singers try out, but no one could make a commitment.

I scraped up some gas money and headed up to Prince George. The guitar player Ron and I had been pretty close friends throughout high school and still chatted from time to time.

I showed up at the old heritage home owned by his family, where he was living and the band was holding tryouts. When I got there, the drummer, another schoolmate and

Ron were there alone jammin' out.

I walked in and Ron said, "hey Mike the lyrics are right here. You wanna sing a few?" I grabbed the lyric sheets, found the song they were jamming to and started singing "Sweet Home Alabama", then on to the next and the next.

After that it wasn't long until things fell into place, and once they let me in on their plans, I joined the band.

Chapter 5

Gunshy

We were just a bunch of young guys in our early 20's.

None of us had "any" experience, with how to run a business, let alone what it would take to control a budget and run a traveling band.

We had no management, no agents at any "professional level" (yet), to help point us in the right direction. Going in dark, but with a ton of great ideas.

Anyone who's started up a business, or followed through on a good idea knows, "These things cost money. And sometimes lots of it."

Fortunately for us (and later unfortunate for them) the parents of the main band founder, provided all the support funding we needed.

This enabling the band to start up a business at the bank.

With a healthy investment at stake, we were set to put together this new country music touring band.

With that secure, now we're on the payroll and time to bring all these killer ideas (big ideas) to fruition.

Name of the band:

The name started off as Hazard County, with the Logo being a sketch of a couple turkey vultures, sitting on a tree branch, like out of an old cartoon.

It was a cool idea, but short lived (I think some other band had the name?)

Then Ron came up with the name Gunshy and it stuck. He wrote a song called, "Rock and Roll Country Boys" which later became the theme for everything Gunshy.

Drums - Gord Lead guitar - Ron

Bass - Jeff, then Terry and lastly Mike (RIP) Keys - Cal

Acoustic - Me

Vocals - Myself and all above

With more than a few bucks invested in the band, the plan was to do things right. I didn't have any cash, but invested a family gift, hoping it would be enough?

Of course, it was a learning process. I'm sure the investors gave the best advice they had from time to time.

But they kept their distance and allowed the guys to learn their way, through good old trial and error.

Ron and I walked into B & B Music on George St. in Prince George, BC. We looked around at guitars, and a cut out blue Takamine caught my eye. He gave me chord charts and showed me where to put my fingers and how to strum. Ron always had an amazing amount of patience teaching me how to play. I played it til my fingers bled. It was the summer of 89... haha

Anyone who's learned how to play guitar at any level, knows that throbbing and aching feeling in your finger tips, day after day until finally, you build up enough calluses to play a full chord without the pain.

First song I ever learned how to play and sing on that guitar was "Killin' Time" by Clint Black.

Fast forward:

After a month or so of feedback issues, I traded the Tak in for a Godin, which I still have.

Okay, back on track:

Time to "build" a tour bus (old school bus) ... But, not just any old school bus.

We cleared out all the seats, then for safety's sake and insurance purposes, installed a metal reinforced wall, to separate us from the area soon to be loaded with gear in the back.

We put comfortable bunks in the rear, then visited a local salvage yard and picked up four nice reclining seats for up front.

We riveted tin over the windows, sanded and buffed it all out and got it ready for paint.

After a total white paint job, a local artist designed the logo.

An American Dukes of Hazard type rebel flag, but with the stars replaced with Canadian maple leafs, to add the Canadian sense of coolness.

Steve hand painted a huge Gunshy logo across both sides of the bus, with bullet holes throughout the lettering. "GUNSHY" above the windshield in large bold letters. It looked pretty damn impressive. The bus was ready to go...

None of us had any clue what a rebel flag meant or represented back then. It just looked cool.

Not too far down the road that Gunshy band logo would be tattooed on some band members (including myself) and even several fans. What a commitment.

Well, time to test out the bus and make a trip to Axe Music in Edmonton, Alberta. Many calls back and forth were made, consulting on what we needed and would set us apart from everyone else currently on the circuit. I think we wanted every advantage possible, to get the best gigs at the best clubs.

Who knew sound gear would play such a significant role?

Everything was actually quite well calculated… Even though we didn't really know for sure, there was some pretty damn good guessing..

Hey, while we're at it, let's visit the country store with the gigantic cowboy boot on the roof and pick out our stage clothes.

What? *They're gunna even buy our stage clothing*? Yup!

Then professional photo shoots were set up to look the part we were shooting for. Young, long hair, all dressed in long rider coats and cowboy hats.

It was like putting together a grown ass boy band.

Unfortunately, still no real solid direction and/or influence from anyone who'd been there before.

I didn't know any better and was definitely going in blind. Had thoughts and ideas of what you'd see in magazines, movies, and TV, but no real experience with any of it.

However, we were following the plan, and it was working.

Here we are in Edmonton (for me the big city) Everyone chose a *Cowboy* hat, which suited them best. We all got matching long rider jackets, western type shirts, bolo ties and why not, "I'll take a pair of those snakeskin boots". Hell, we had matching outfits for every night of the week.

A warehouse was rented down off 1st Ave. in an industrial area. Lots of space for setups, teardown and tweaking all the gear.

The cool, old character home, living room is no longer our rehearsal spot. It's just a place to sleep and eat.

We set up our brand new JBL P/A system with loads of QSC power, 24 channel board, drum riser, and all the bands stage gear. Everything surrounded by an impressive light show.

"No dead air man."

We all had set lists in front of us on monitors, and if no mistakes were made, we'd keep going until we were done the set. Then take a break, like we were live in a club.

Typical Set List:

Sweet home Alabama Killin' Time

Mirror Mirror

Boot Scootin' Boogie

Storms Never Last

Walk Softly

Chatahoochie

Friends In Low Place Sold

Hillbilly Rock

The Race is On

Mercury Blues

The set lists were current and well rounded (at first) After all, we weren't your typical country band. We were a rock band with a country singer.

We worked out our four set song lists, each comprised of 10 or so songs, and rehearsed, as though we were playing in front of a crowded bar.

Back in those days the clubs expected four, 40 minute sets, starting at 9:00pm ending at 2:00 am. Playing Monday to Saturday. 6 nights a week of live entertainment.

We'd have friends and family come by the warehouse to see the band's progress from time to time (family during the day, friends at night). Things were tightening up. Our promo packs were out with the booking agent and the clubs started filling up our calendar.

Chapter 6

Time to Hit the Road

Tour dates for several weeks in advance are booked. First stop Hanna, and we hit the road.

Arrive in Hanna the night prior, get to our hotel and settle in for night. I remember feeling quite excited.

In the early afternoon, we parked the bus outside the club, opened the back door of the bus and started unloading gear.

The club doors were opened for us to haul in the gear and set up the stage. At the entrance of the club hangs an "8 x 10" photo of Gunshy which stood out from other promo.

A couple young guys were hanging around asking questions, while we unloading the bus. Turns out they had a band and invited us to a party one night.

Many years later, that young group found major success.

As for us:

Time to set up the stage, like we did in the warehouse.

Metal trusses with tons of chrome lights. Gel inserts with red, magenta, pink, blue, yellow, and clear colors matching each side of the stage. The front and back also covered with more trusses and lights.

A black Gunshy backdrop covering the massive collection of wires, running to the distro box for the lights.

The stage was set, and it "looked" like we were great.

Back to the band house to have a quick rest. Everyone grabs a bite, then cleans up and dresses for the night.

To this point no one other than our parents and some local friends, had heard the band live. Of course *they* thought we were great.

We pull up in front of the club.

Everyone inside the bus is dressed in sharp matching getups.

Stepping down off the bus, one black, long rider jacket after the next, carrying our axe cases followed by one with a drum bag. We single file our way one by one, through the crowd and into the club.

It was a Monday night, there was a line-up out the door. As we're walking past the crowd, people are buzzing…

It was a small town and maybe all our promo hype had some folks excited? I hear a fella say, "these guys are killer." How he knew was beyond me, cause we hadn't even played yet…

However, it provoked a confidence, we were doing things right. Even if, to this point, it was only smoke and mirrors.

In fairness: We were a group of good looking young guys, long hair, all dressed alike, with a ton of energy.

Upbeat tunes rocking the stage one tune smoothly flowing into the next…

Our song list was current and kept the beer swillin', whiskey drinkin' patrons dancin', and engaged all night.

For some of us, it was the first time we'd ever seen line dancing and two stepping.

The energy rolled from the first song, right thru to the last Saturday night encore. Our first club gig was a hit, and our fan base began.

Our first opening opportunity:

I recall leaving Brandon, Manitoba right after our Saturday night tear down. Loaded up all our gear in the bus and travelled non stop for 24+ hours after losing to the time change, before hitting Prince George, BC.

Along the way, I remember waking and walking up to the driver. It was a blizzard outside, and I could hardly see the lines on the road. The driver said, "it's been like this for an hour or so". I said, "dude, you're going pretty fast man. Maybe you should slow down a bit."

As he slowed down, the blizzard started to clear and we saw the row of red lights in front of us. Turns out he'd been tailgating a semi the entire time.

We swapped out so he could get some rest. It was our first hometown gig, and we were opening for a popular band on the radio at the time.

Maybe we got the gig because we had all the gear they required, but how cool was that. There was an odd excitement in the air.

A few of us guys in the band, were standing in a line up at a taco place across from The Cadillac Ranch, taking a late lunch break during set up. One of our band guys says to another, *this gig is gunna be packed.* Everyone's coming to see us, they're not even here to see the headliner".

I recognized the next two people in the line up as the headliners and felt a disgusted feeling of shame. Really man, we think that much of ourselves already?

When we got back to the club (or as we were leaving the taco place) I remember saying, "dude you know that was the band behind us in line hey?" Response was a shrug off?

Funny how little things like that can stick around so vividly, yet so many good times are forgotten? Guess I just never wanted to be that guy, or, maybe I took it out of context? It was our first local gig in front of our hometown friends and family. And sometimes people just say stupid shit.

The club was jam packed. The headliner killed their set and left immediately afterward. The Cadillac Ranch stayed hopping, as we closed out the night.

And, the tour continues:

Lethbridge, High River, Wainwright, Red Deer, Calgary, Edmonton, Hinton, Edson, Drayton Valley, Whitecourt, Grand Cache, Grande Prairie, Fairview, Peace River, and High Level, Alberta.

Fort St. John, Prince George, Vancouver, Abbotsford, Surrey, Whalley, Chilliwack, and Nanaimo BC.

North Battleford, Prince Albert, Moose Jaw, Regina and Saskatoon. Saskatchewan. Brandon and Winnipeg Manitoba.

Clubs:

Cadillac Ranch, Viva's, The Silver Spur, Silverados, The Wild West, Ranchman's, The Texas Bull, Shilo's, Trac's and Kelly's, Yukatan's, Poncho and Lefty's, JR Country, Wichita North and more.

Days turned into weeks, weeks into months…

Over a couple years, we've created quite a buzz and have earned a decent level of small town fame.

The local newspaper photographers would show up to the clubs, then run a story the next day.

There were great clubs and not so great clubs. A Rooms and B Rooms. The class of club would often determine the type of accommodations.

There were more than enough live music venues to go around. If you were a decent enough band, you stayed busy.

Gunshy was becoming a bigger draw and getting more and more popular by the week...

We definitely weren't as talented as "The Underground Outlaws" or "Rocking Horse" bands, but our look and vibe was gaining us momentum.

Most clubs were one week gigs, some were two. The two week gigs gave us a leisure day to go do our own thing.

I recall playing snooker at local pool halls, and the band using the opportunity to learn/rehearse new songs.

The Silver Spur:

Early on one night, a bar room brawl breaks out. The band lays down their instruments and jumps in to help out the staff.

There were bodies flying around the bar, then out the door.

Some short-lived excitement, then a fella walks in... approaches the bar and has the server line up the stage with shooters.

The stage wasn't very deep, but it was very long (that's what she said). Between songs the band would take a shot.

Shot after shot, after shot...

At some point during or after a break, our drummer lost a shoe somewhere, so we ask the bartender who'd been Rocking Horse's drummer, to take his place for the last set or so.

We had wireless headset mic's and for some reason, I recall singing a song or two while lying on my back? I Believe it was a weekday, and the entire bar was in on the shenanigans. Very likely the only time something like that happened??

The Band House:

May have also happened after the night above...

One of the guys struggles to put the key in the front door of the band house. Another standing on the steps looks down at the welcome mat in front of the door and says, "hey, don't they call these throw rugs?" He threw the mat out into the front yard, as the door opens.

Encouraged by the throw rug, another guy throws something else out of the house, taking turns back and forth.

I go to bed... Guess this went on all night, cause when we got up the next morning, the entire living room and kitchen was staged and set up outside. Maybe even one of the guys still passed out on a mattress? Chairs around the kitchen table with plates and cutlery. Living room couch and chair, set up with the TV and stand. Was very creative.

A missed opportunity?:

The place was hoppin' and the drinks were flowing while playing live to radio, at a popular Vancouver night club "JR Country". The guys disappear after a set, for a hit off an unfiltered cigarette (which they'd do from time to time). I'm flying solo when approached by a well dressed professional looking gentleman. We engaged in a bit of small talk, he told me his name, and who he represented. I forgot his name seconds later, but knew he was a big deal.

It was around the height of our band's hype.

He was curious, asking rapid questions. After a bit, our break was ending and we're going back live to radio. So, this fella passes me his card.

When on stage I handed it to the band leader...

Recently, I was reminded that the card went into the band's book of business cards and that's where it remained.

The card: it was an A and R guy from a Major Record Label. At this point, I was still just along for the ride and will never know if a call was ever made?

"If Only" doesn't matter any more. However, it makes for a cool story.

Club doors opened up, to allow the smoke out when the fog machine ran a tad long... "Smoke."

Back then, there were no indoor smoking restrictions. Everyone smoked so much, most clubs didn't require a fog machine for that foggy stage effect from the lights.

Chapter 7

Hiccups

Well, with popularity, comes downfalls I guess. Of course, things could've gotten a lot better, but we didn't know any different. Everything has it's defining moments.

Things they would've done differently, if given the chance. "I'd Do it Over Again" Honestly most memories with Gunshy were pretty damn cool.

But, stupid one sided arguments got in my way, both in life and with the band. Gunshy walks into a club in Grande Prairie, Alberta on a Friday or Saturday night and makes our way to the stage.

They had strippers during the day, so the table full of riggers had been there since lunch time.

When walking to that stage, someone makes a comment about the stylish overalls one of us was wearing...

The overalls were cool and the guy was in *a band.*
They continued with some heckling. We're on stage with mic's in front of us, so maybe we yapped back a bit, which didn't improve the situation. On break, the rest of the band takes off to their rooms, as I head to the bar for a mug of OJ and soda.

A guy from the table approaches me along the way, with another buddy close behind. He gets in my face, then out of nowhere, my brother-in-law (at the time) walks up behind me and says, *hey, is there a fucking problem here?* Ha ha, best timing ever!

My sister, brother and his wife showed up shortly after, and the rest of the night went off without a hitch. Other than giving my brother and his wife my room and spending the night, in a hotel lobby chair.

Which brings us to a gig the following week, at Shiloh's in Red Deer.

The drummer approaches me and says, "the club in Grande Prairie said, they ain't booking us again, if we bring the Indian with us." Continues with, "So, we're gunna book the gig without you and you'll have to find your way back for the following week".

What... I just remember seeing red and saying "F@#! you, I'm done". I gave my two weeks notice and threw a chair across the dance floor. Finished that week in Red Deer, and the next in Ft. Saint John, then parted ways.

Prior to my exit:
The drum kit had been set up in the center of the stage with trusses carrying the mic's stands upside down from the ceilings.

However cool the idea, the drum kit being center stage wasn't always practical and created sound issues. So, I guess it was short lived.

I'm living in Kamloops, and I get a call from the drummer's dad asking if I'd like to go to work with him?

I said, "Of course man, when do I start?" I worked through the next few weeks laying tiles at Gold's Gym.

He was a cool guy, had tunes on while we worked. He had toured himself, playing drums with a recording band, many years prior.

One day he says, " Hey Mike you can expect a call from Gunshy, with an offer to go back and play again with the band.

We all still had our private lives going on.

I'm 26 and married. Had a beautiful little girl who owned my heart, and it was always tough being away from her.

Even though I was just another hired gun, I had hopes that the band would reach the next level, and good things would happen down the road.

I was now making an extra $100 per week, standing center stage, and singing more songs.

I didn't care much about the stage position and song count, but the extra money was helpful.

Differences were shaken off with booking a different club, in place of the one that didn't want me there. So, I was set to make another go at it...

Most bands had their hiccups and ours was no different. During my brief absence there was another band conflict, and we'd lost our bass player.

I happened to know a guy in Kamloops. I called him up and turns out he was available.

So, we both headed to Prince George together, and Gunshy was back on the road.

Terry and his wife recently brought their boat over to our dock this past summer, and I reminded him of when he used to play his bass (as a piano solo), while the drummer sang "Imagine".

At this point, there's still no collective band decisions being made. From my perspective on the inside looking in, one guy was in control, and it wasn't the guy whose parents made the financial investment.

I sang and did my *job*.

More changes were made, with another new bass player coming out of Vancouver, but this time he came with a keyboard player as well. I believe they were our guitar player's brothers' roommates.

I became good friends with these guys. I guess we were the outsiders (even though I'd been in the band from the get-go).

These guys came with a lot of experience from different rock bands.

Rock bands didn't earn what country bands were making back then, so a lot of rock bands started playing country.

And, we weren't much different. With all the changes, we were pretty much a rock band with a country singer.

The new guys were natural performers filled with ch

arisma and energy, bringing the band to that next level.

Now, we're showing up in a stretched out white Lincoln (looked impressive pulling up in front of the clubs), with a matching bus. There were boxes and boxes of Gunshy t-shirts of all sizes and a ton of hats for merch.

After a while, it seemed like we had walking billboards everywhere.

Not sure at what point, but we all made the Garth Brooks switchover, from regular Shure 58's in mic stands, to wireless headsets.

Night after night we were walking across tables playing and singing, from all areas of the bar. Sometimes we even hit the dance floor with our own, non-typical choreographed dance moves.

Our drummer is now booking the band directly and through an agent, while still collecting payments, paying us players. and handling any cash transactions.

Seemed the band was doing well financially? Now we have a sound guy and drum tech, a light tech and merch sales, also swapping off as drivers.

We had a crew, (well, the drummer had a crew) and they did all the set ups. Us side guys only had to show up for sound check.

Regardless, the band must be doing alright, cause, guess who's recording an album?

Rock And Roll Country Boys:

Gunshy was getting ready to record it's first album "Rock and Roll Country Boys".

The band had a quick break in the action. I took the opportunity to go home and see my little girl.

Meanwhile, the band (drummer, guitar player and road crew) rented out, renovated, and furnished a large home in Surrey.

A few girls from back east made the move also. I imagine to help out with the rent... After a short visit home, I went back to the coast and stayed with my wife's sister and

her boyfriend (he was a bass player in a rock band).

While the band guys and crew were still finishing up reno's at their rental and setting up the studio recording plans, I ran sound for the rock band, to help earn my keep.

I don't recall being included in any of the recording conversations of who, what, when, and where, but there was a plan. I was just hanging around waiting.

Although there was inner band conflict going on, all the guys pulled together still hoping for a future.

Any songs written for the album, whether it was independently penned, or a collective write, everyone in Gunshy was credited for each song:

Rock and Roll Country Boys Country Woman

Hey, Truck Driver Lost Without You Just Baby To Me You Got Me Runnin'

Cover Of The Rolling Stone (Dr. Hook)

There were a few more, but I can't remember off hand and don't own a copy. The album was recorded in Vancouver with Dale Penner, as Producer.

We played the songs in clubs after recording and they went over very well.

There was so much time, money, effort, and hopes leading up to this recording. The anticipation was building like a city skyscraper.

But there was also something else building, and that was more and more conflict within the band. And of course, some of us had our own relationship issues outside the band as well.

For me the anticipation turned into total uncertainty, being pulled every which way.

The band seemed to have no real collective direction at all? So, it was time I stepped aside...

Within the short timeframe after recording, the band continued to battle with its inner issues. The guys tried keeping things together, but ultimately through my eyes, the one-sided decision making continued, and finally became its demise.

And so, the Gunshy era was no more...

The highly anticipated "Rock and Roll Country Boys" album was an unfortunate miss of irreconcilable differences and was never mastered or released.

I did have a meeting with the original investor, offering me the album and recording rights. But I obviously didn't have that kind of cash. And, there was no way I could get the band up and going again on my own, without a pile of dough.

In the end, sure things weren't perfect. But, was it an amazing once in a lifetime experience? Absofuckinglutely!

Singing wirelessly, from a chuck wagon swinging over a packed dance floor at Kelly's, slammed clubs Monday thru Saturday nights, with loyal fans following us from city to city showing their support. Bar room brawls, after parties, local fame with each town we played. High end corporate gigs and rodeos. It was like being a star character in one of your all time favorite movies.

Movie scene:

A group of Beer pin up girls dancing stage front in Daisy Dukes and bikini tops. My snakeskin boot propped on top a monitor, mic in hand belting out a tune. One starts, then another, they're kissing and licking that snakeskin boot like a scene out of a Rock and Roll movie.

Those boots were never the same again...

It was a fun chapter, hanging out and partying with some of the finest humans out there.

And, the cherry on top of it all, finding another beautiful daughter in the mix, after all the madness.

The protector, my Inner Music voice, gently whispered... "It's not over"

With Gunshy a thing of the past, life moves on. I've moved back to Prince George with my wife and daughter, and we now had new twin boys.

Chapter 8

Bulletproof

Family was priority, so I rented a home with Metis Housing and worked as one of their maintenance men.

Over the next few years the kids were growing. I burned the candle at both ends, working full time during the day, getting home and hanging out with the kids until bedtime, then head out and play six nights a week at the clubs and weekends in the pubs.

I'd get home after two am, change some diapers, feed the twins, sleep a few hours and get up to repeat it all again, just like Groundhog Day.

Bulletproof:

A real live country band. Haha!

Man, I loved this band. A great friend Merle on guitar, his dad Bob on steel, with Rick & Rick on Bass and drums.

It's come full circle, cause my buddy Rick on Bass & vocals was to be the original singer for Gunshy. "Someone I respect for still being out there killin' it".

We played all the local clubs and pubs in Prince George for a couple years and were well liked by management, staff, and patrons.

Everyone had lives going on and really, just enjoyed playing music.

I stayed at the Cadillac Ranch (Old Rock Pit) band house during a break up. Was a nice little bachelor pad by the pool.

The more than generous band house owner, had a musician boyfriend from one of the road bands. Eventually he turned that little pad into a pretty cool recording studio.

The first ever recording out of that studio was an eclectic album of mine of old classics like; Under the Boardwalk, On the Dark Side, Only You, Shame Shame Shame Shame, Moody Blue, You Never Can Tell, Tears in Heaven and others.

It was quite convenient, cause every week we had a different band staying at the house. We knew guys in all the bands coming and going.

Everyone was always curious what we were doing and when asked, they were always willing to help out with the project. Mike and Cal from Gunshy (at the time playing in different bands) played on the project as well. Guys from several different road bands, including the band I was in at the time "Bulletproof".

All instruments and even back up vocals came from a lot of different bands members and friends over the years. I loved being involved in the build, wiring that studio, then being it's first project. I still have the CD today.

My wife makes a decision to move to Penticton BC, where her parents had recently moved. I follow suit and head south.

I find work in construction, building the Kettle Valley Railway Station through an employment insurance program, in Summerland. Later I help out a brother-in-law hanging eavestroughs, then several construction jobs to keep afloat.

Other than the odd jam session at the father-in-law's Army & Navy Club, there wasn't much music. Just voices louder than my inner music, keeping me off the right track.

The kids were growing up fast. I spent most of my time working and being a dad. We had a rocky marriage throughout, and it finally ended for good after our gazillionth breakup.

The kids were around 8-10 and they lived between their mother and I for a year or so.

A long distance relationship developed between my younger daughter's mother and

I, and they made a trip to come visit us, where we all got acquainted.

Irish twin daughters and identical twin boys. Soon after that visit, I put together a plan, rented a two bedroom apartment, loaded up my truck and a trailer and moved to Edmonton, spending time between their place and mine.

My girlfriend entered me into "The Country Vocal Spotlight".

Apparently, it was a pretty big deal in Alberta, with contestants coming from all over the province to compete in a vocal contest.

I'm in my late 30's at this point.

The old guy, sings a song and moves on to the next round of the contest...

I was coming off a music hiatus of many years, but still had a lot more maturity and experience than the others.

There was some snotty cattiness coming from a couple of the older judges making me feel guilty, but the thought of dropping out soon passed, with the support of the organizer and President of the Country Vocal Spotlight ("CVS').

I kept hanging in there, round after round, until it came down to the finals.

We were hopeful, but truly didn't expect the judges would let me beat out the young guy?

When it was announced that I was the Grand Prize Winner for my category, I was truly shocked and surprised.

The prize package had a trip to Nashville, Tennessee, including another opportunity to compete in a North American vocal competition in Pigeon Forge, plus artist management, performance dates at major events throughout the city of Edmonton, Lammle's clothing, tickets to music week and awards shows, Merle Haggard concert tickets, and several gigs throughout the province.

I'll be forever grateful for that opportunity. It allowed me a brand new start, at a late age, for another go in the Country Music Industry/Business...

Time to cash in on the big CVS contest win. With a lot of media coverage and spotlights on this new achievement, the feelers went out.

I managed to land a couple sponsorships, and good things started to happen.

My oldest daughter was turning 12 and old enough to make her own decision, which parent she wanted to live with. She moved to Edmonton and into the apartment with me. A few months later, we rented a house big enough for all of us, and the boys moved to Edmonton as well.

A life long family friend who loved music, helped sponsor a four song EP. I spent a ton of time playing guitar and writing songs.

When the time came and I was ready, we found Gary at Beta Studios in Edmonton and together we produced a fantastic four song EP. It was such a great experience.

And fortunately, it was in my hands before the trip to Nashville.

1 One of A Kind
2 Lovin' You
3 Caroline
4 Picture Daddy With You

CAMA's 2004 Best Country Album

Off to Nashville Tennessee. And soon to be headed into Pigeon Forge Tennessee for the North American Country Music Associations' International Vocal Competition.

My runner-up was invited along as well. "My lil' bro Aaron Goodvin, has moved on to be a very talented multi award winning success story, and I follow his career and voice to this day". The flight over was filled with young excitement and anticipation. The youngest male winner walks to the front of the plane and approaches a flight attendant...

Next thing you know he's on the plane's microphone introducing our group. He calls us all up and we break into a rendition of "Will the Circle be Unbroken".

From that day on, there was never a doubt in my mind, that kid (Brett Kissel) would go on to be one of Canada's biggest names in country music -...

We land in Nashville Tennessee.

My father had a joke. He'd say, *my boy's going to Nashville*, then add, *yeah, the walk'll do him good* and break into laughter... Always a joker (in a good way).

The NACMAI (North American Country Music Association International). That was pretty exciting right, to be in a big competition in the U.S. of A., and Tennessee to boot. I was just a hop, skip, and song from Nashville, and there was a huge auditorium of people watching contestants from across the U.S.

Winner: Mike Gouchie

The NACMAI's "2004 International Male Vocalist Of The Year" Adult Traditional Country.

Everyone in our group took home hardware for winning their categories. Our Canadian CVS group proudly wandered lower Broadway over the next few days.

Kids were welcome in the clubs during the day, so they took every opportunity possible, to jump on a stage for a song or two, including the World Famous "Tootsies".

As a group, we visited all the Country Music hot spots.

When I walked across the stage of the Grand Ole Opry, *the goose bumps slowly start to dissipate as the names and voices of those who stood there before me, flooded my body with a calm nostalgia.*

The seats may have been empty while I was standing in front of that old iconic microphone, but I was lost in the moment and singing for a packed house.

Heading back to Edmonton

We were headed home on Air Canada when the one and only Bill Borgwart, Alberta's Hall of Fame photographer who had been snapping shots all over Nashville for the CVS, approached me and said, *"Mike, look at the airplane's country music playlist"*. I looked, and there it was, "Picture Daddy With You". I remember being very laid back on the outside but feeling super excited on the inside. Here I was listening to a song I wrote through a set of $5.00 airplane headphones. And that entire time I was thinking of the inspiration behind the song and looking forward to seeing them all (with G Ma and Grampa Gouchie) when we got home.

It was all happening fast--yet it had taken forever. I had moved to Edmonton, I was in a supportive relationship, I won a contest and recorded an EP, then I went to Nashville, and I won another contest. And on top of that, I won another contest with a secondary record label out of Winnipeg.

The prize was a recording deal. But at the time, I had other recording plans in progress. So, I made arrangements with the label out of Winnipeg, to allow my brother to take my place for the record, which all worked out....

Now, Maryanne Gibson (CVS/GCHF) is my current manager and to this day, was and is, the most supportive, honest, true hearted country music personality, I've ever met in the industry.

We were moving forward and I kept focused on recording in Nashville, while still making appearances with Global Country's CVS, going from event to event.

I sang my version of the National Anthem in Edmonton with 20,000 spectators at a Canadian Rodeo Finals, *"Oh Canada, your home's on native land"*. There wasn't any media mention, but there were quite a few who approached me later with a chuckle.

I flew out to Toronto, where "One of A Kind" won the 2004 Best Country Album at the Canadian Aboriginal Music Awards. I had never seen anything like it before. Being there in the presence of all these artists, dressed in their regalia, they brought me to tears several times. There was something so special about their stunning performances.

"It was the first time I'd been surrounded by people of my own culture, celebrating and being rewarded for their accomplishments."

This helped create more buzz and kept me busy flying around to corporate events.

But, never keeping me away from home for more that a few days at a time.

The pay was $1,500, $3,000 or $5,000+ all dependent on whether I did the show alone, brought guitar accompaniment or brought a full band? There were flights, accommodations and per diems playing a role, and of course, fuel costs if travelling on wheels.

Big Valley Jamboree was a great gig. 2004 Main Stage had Brad Paisley, Reba, Lonestar, Ricky Skaggs, Leann Rimes along with Canadian Artists Doc Walker, Aaron Pritchett, Jason McCoy, Brad Johner and many up and comers.

That year my gig was in the BVJ Songwriters Tent. The Song writing circles have always been a favourite of mine. It's where you get to tell your song's story and hear others, sharing theirs. The following year I performed as well (Big and Rich on Main Stage). I never had anything scripted and usually just spoke what was on my mind at the time. Their big hit "Save a Horse Ride a Cowboy" was still on heavy radio rotation, so I shocked a tent full of folks when I said, "yeah Big and Rich stole my song and changed the words.

Mine were Save a Moose Ride an Indian". Most laughed, although I think some were scared since this was when saying "Indian" became a negative/derogatory statement.

My name was getting out. A couple of my songs have been released to radio and picked up by a few reporting stations and lots of secondary stations. This was good, and above par for the course.

I'm busy sending out emails and trying to find sponsorships for the real deal. A full length Nashville recorded album, complete with all the hidden costs that go with that kind of deal.

The struggle was real, but I kept moving forward. I always tried to keep myself involved and as current as possible, with everything related to the music industry.

I remember being selected as a juror with Canada Council and Factor. The task, choosing successful grant applications in Country music categories. And, it was a great learning process.

It's funny, at the time I didn't really think to much about it, but years later with time to reflect, I saw so much more. Four of us sat around a large table, chairs spaced quite far apart. They chose me and one other person from the Association to hand out the applicant's packages.

We handed the packages and then the jurors stacked them in the order they chose from left to right.

There was some discomfort until the jurors figured out that no one had any real connection to the music business end of things. Once we all figured that out the tension lessened and we all started collaborating, sharing thoughts and having a bit of fun.

I may have baited the panel a bit with comments like, *man, just think how hard it is for an independent artist to make it, without the support of these grants*. It worked though and slowly I was convincing the others to take more time and dig deeper into the applications. It was good to see them leaning towards hard work and dedication, rather than popularity.

Looking back on a couple of those unknown artists now, it's gratifying to think we may have played a small role, in moving them forward into what are now successful music careers.

* * *

My first EP had received some great accolades and paved the road for what was to happen next.

My sister put me in touch with a very successful businessman she knew. He was a great guy and had a lot going on, so I was grateful for his time and kindness. His help and connections were going to be invaluable.

He invited me to his home (largest log home in the world). So, I drove up and brought along my guitar. There were a few guests as well and after showing me around his beautiful home and my sleeping quarters, it was time for dinner.

His personal chef prepared an amazing meal. They talked and I mostly listened.

Shortly after dinner I brought out my guitar to entertain his dinner guests. One guest in particular was a big country fan and shared stories of concerts he'd been to and artists he'd seen.

I was surprised to find out that he and our host had been in prior discussions, regarding a potential sponsorship through a major health product he owned. Everything seemed to fit together perfectly.

Before long, I was sharing my plans for a Nashville recorded album. This led to talks about making music videos, sparing no expense.

I felt like everyone around me had a strong belief in where my future was heading, and I don't recall any large amounts of alcohol being consumed.

With a solid sponsor for the new album, I made another quick trip back to Nashville for more writing sessions and some recording connections.

I spent most of my time writing and meeting writers. Some publishing companies have you on the clock, an hour with this one, then an hour with another. For them, it's a job and just a normal day…

The crazy plan I had in my head, for when I became a well enough known artist, was I'd put out a full album of nothing but my own songs. My thoughts were that as an established artist, it would land me more radio airplay, which I could later cash in on it through royalties.

There were so many goals and strategies, swirling around in my mind, but I was still learning and believed my ideas were becoming more educated.

Before and/or after writing sessions, I was still knocking on all the other doors of music row.

It's a much tougher chore as a new independent artist trying to find great songs in this new era, than it would be if you're hooked up to a known label and/or management company.

The yesterdays are gone.

I'm an old soul and think I'd have stood a better chance, back when talent was being discovered. But, here I am caught in the struggle of trying to buy my way in. No one is looking for talent anymore, it's all sheeple flocking to the stables.

More and more things were turning to who you knew and how much money you're bringing to the table. The elite get first kick at the can, and that's just how the world works. If you want to be taken seriously, you'd best have a strong sense of belonging. So, although I was a no one in Nashville, I brought a solid mindset and a positive attitude each and every time.

Selection Process:

Every 100 songs or so pitched, there'd be one I'd say, *I'll sing the hell out of this one* and put it in a special pile.

It's a long process to find what you want. Especially if you're going to listen to every lyric of every song that's pitched your way.

So, after a while, you come up with your own system.

For me it didn't matter if the writer was well know or not, I gave every song a fair shot, cause you just never know?

Some demos get clicked to the next track pretty quick, but with catchy intro's, the ear stays a little longer. If it has a good hook and strong bones, that one definitely gets a full listen.

If everything about a song catches me, I put it aside and go through again and again.

So after a few months of going through pitches I made my choices.

Every hit songwriter has that first song. And, for every great song, there's another 100 they'd call average. Sure they get a lot of cuts, but the hits don't happen every day.

Always chase the songs and not the writer.

If I didn't write a song myself, I did my best to choose it for the right reasons.

Not every song has to be a hit, but if it's special and means something to me, I'm happy with that.

Just no fillers. (songs picked for the sake of filling up a project) At the end of the day, believe in your choices...

Moral of the story:

Don't just go to Nashville, pick some songs and record an album that day... Cause, that's just stupid.

Unless, you have a pile of money and just wanna have some fun... Then have fun.

Well, I could keep writing about song writing scenarios, but now that I've got songs to record (including a couple solid keepers I penned myself), I'm that much closer. The new CD project, to be recorded in Nashville, was real.

* * *

I'd previously been introduced to a producer, and I'd done my research and trusted his resume. He seemed sincerely excited about my record and a deal was struck. Soon he had all the recording details in place and we were ready to go.

Time to fly back to Nashville and put all the planning into action. I had all my ducks in a row, everything meticulously planned out (so I thought).

Here I am:

Everything I had previously set out to accomplish, was now in motion.

I land back in Nashville and head to the same *creature of habit* hotel, I'd stayed at before, but this time the vibe is different.

The previous trips were usually filled with excitement and jitters. *who might I get to write with, or meet? What killer song am I gunna write, or find?*

I'm feeling what I'd call, *surprisingly calm* as I walk into Sound Emporium (a major

Nashville Recording Studio) with my folder of songs.

There's a soundboard stretching from one side of a massive room to the other, and huge walls of glass, partitioning off the sound room from the spaces on the other side. There's other smaller rooms within that large room. The smaller rooms are insulated with glass windows facing the sound room, for isolating instruments or vocals being recorded.

In the middle, there's a large open room with high end gear. Everything is spaced out strategically to give each player their own space.

Each of these spaces are filled with guys who've played on some of the biggest Nashville recordings of all time. Guitar, bass, drums, keyboard.

They all have Nashville numbered charts *of my songs* sitting in front of them, all ready to lay down some world class tracks.

Standing in an isolated vocal booth singing, I begin looking out into the middle of this room.

A warmth of overwhelming confidence floods my ears, as the sounds of world class musicians fill my headphones.

I feel humbly reserved but taken back by their compliments. It felt so rewarding having these *cool cats* throwing props. I still had a lot of hard work to put in, but I felt like respect was being earned.

When you're in the moment, there's really not a lot of time to reflect, and/or truly take it all in.

It's crazy looking back... I was in a studio with gold and platinum records hanging off its walls, while world class Nashville players, were laying down tracks on "my" record.

For the first time, I finally felt like I belonged. My *music voice* was telling me, *we're home.*

Most instrument tracks were laid down at the Sound Emporium studio, along with scratch vocals. The steel guitar tracks were done at a private home and final vocals mixing and mastering would be done back in Edmonton.

The next day, I called my sponsor to let him know how things are going and to set up payment, but I can't get hold of him and find out from the hook up, that his mother just passed away.

I'm feeling super disrespectful calling him at this time, asking for money. There's just no way. So, I leave a message with condolences thinking, he'll call when he finds time. But the call never came.

Now I'm in Nashville fresh off a recording, and I need to solve a problem. I know I'm going to figure it out, but out of respect, I tell the producer and assure him I'm working on things and should have things cleared up by morning.

Oh, ye of little faith...

First thing in the morning. My mind isn't quite there yet, for any split second thinking that is. It was a long night making calls and I didn't get a whole lot of sleep...

The Call:

I'm waking up, in my reasonably priced Best Western Hotel room. Was my usual go to spot, just off the roundabout by Music Row and just a short jaunt to Lower Broadway. By no means was it the Ritz, but it had a quiet little singer/songwriter lounge where I met some great old fella's, who'd written some big hits back in their day. It was more my speed and I preferred it to the downtown hustle.

Anywho, back to the call...

Me: Hello

Caller: Is this Mike Gouchie? Me: Yes, it is...

Caller: This is your producer's manager (in a rough movie gangster type voice) calling from New York.

Me: How's it going...

Caller: You tell me. I hear you have an outstanding debt? Caller: Let me tell you how we do things around here.

Caller: I've got people here who are gunna come pay you a visit if you don't pay up immediately.

Caller: I don't care how you do it, just do it.

Caller: You hearing me? I can find you. Consider yourself warned. Caller: "We'll" be in touch... CLICK

The night prior I had already made a call and had things arranged for a deposit the next morning, but I wasn't given the chance to respond.

Someone was likely watching too many old gangster flicks.

Obviously, I felt bad that the funding didn't work out the way it was planned. But, to that point all was running perfectly smooth. I just thought I'd be straight up in case there was a problem (which there wasn't) down the road.

So again, I kept my chin up and had to believe in the process...

Losing faith in the producer, I called him up and told him about the phone call I'd received.

He says, *yeah he's looking for his cut*. Really? FFS

Who knows, something else could've been up, but now I'm thinking I chose the wrong guy.

He flicks off the threat, squinting at me with one lazy eye through his glasses, "Let's finish up this album"

The respect factor (regardless of who he had on his resume) was now gone. But, I still had an album to finish and was in it alone.

I call my fiancé and fill her in on the stick.

Once I got through a brief vent, we had a chuckle (more me) about the New York call and continued on, with a nice *adult conversation*.

We talked about how her and the kids were doing, then what my next few days looked like.

At the time she happened to be multitasking and going through the mail.

Says, "there's an envelope with your name on it from the Alberta Foundation for the Arts". I asked her to open it.

It was a grant cheque for $10,000 in support of my new recording.

What? Haha Bonus. I had applied for the grant a few months earlier and it couldn't have come at a more perfect time.

"Okay, maybe if I'd known a few days earlier, it would've saved the New York gangster drama." But, then I wouldn't have this stupid, yet cool, story to tell.

Always staying positive, no matter the situation. Even if I wasn't, I acted though I was.

She went to the bank and I made another call regarding the loan. Was nice I didn't have to borrow as much as I previously thought.

However, because the sponsorship fell through, it did take a few years of instalments to finally pay off that debt. But for me, it was about keeping my word. And I did.

Back to Edmonton:

"Let's get back to work." We still had vocals to finish up...

The Producer takes a hit of his devil's lettuce, then a sip of his gin and says, "Man your voice sounds so good. We don't need any more takes on this one".

This went on track after track... After a short time, we were done.

He told me, "it'll sound a lot more authentic, if we leave it the way it is".

To make things better, I hired my young local friends from the CVS group to come in, lay down some vocal tracks to help me sound better. And, they all killed it.

Now the mixing process. No matter what, a guy is feeling pretty damn good about recording a new Nashville Album. In fairness, the producer was a little old school, and I think he truly thought it was great. And, everything was great. There was just something missing in my vocals.

I had higher expectations, but maybe it was just my performance?

Gallery

Mike Gouchie on tour with George Jones

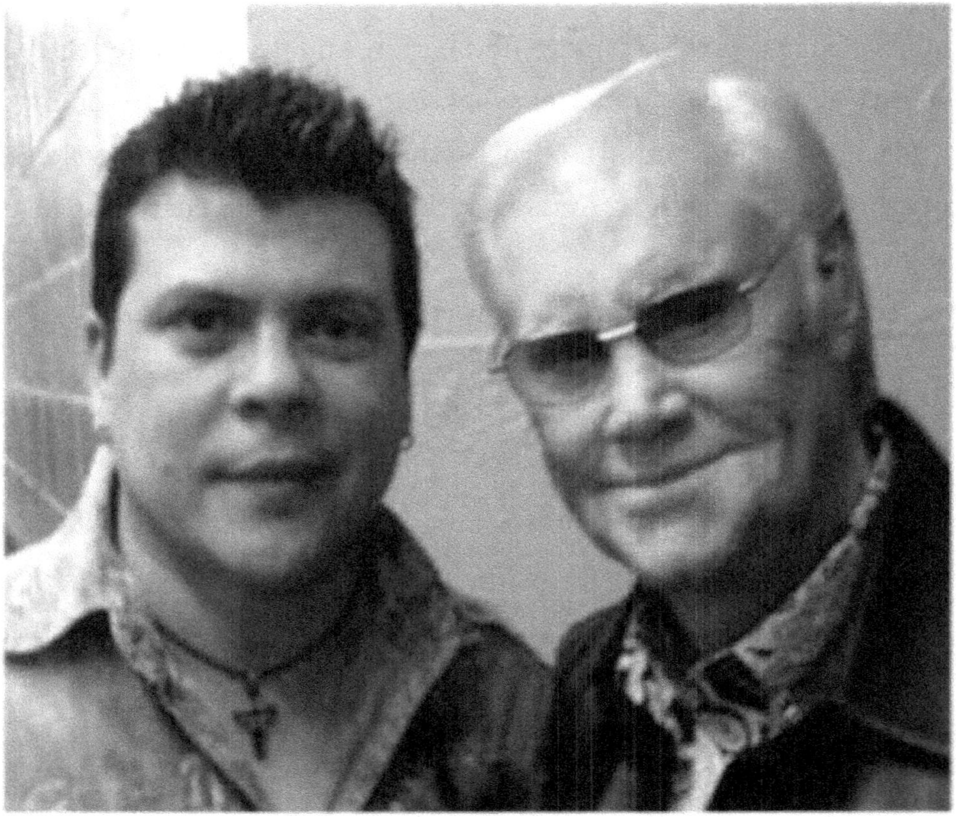

Memories from George Jones tour

George Jones signing guitar and On Stage

Brent Shindell and Linda Kidder on the George Jones tour with Mike Gouchie

Mike Gouchie at awards show with Michael Ohman and Peter Padden

Halifax Nova Scotia appearance with Alan Jackson

THE NEW YORK TIMES BESTSELLER
NEW MATERIAL for the paperback edition!
I Lived to Tell It All
GEORGE JONES

MIKE GOUCHIE
Bad Boys & Angels

Plucked
MIKE GOuCHIE
Angels Unaware
CMT

COUNTRY MUSIC NEWS
THE VOICE OF COUNTRY MUSIC IN CANADA
MIKE GOUCHIE - THE DREAM NEVER DIES

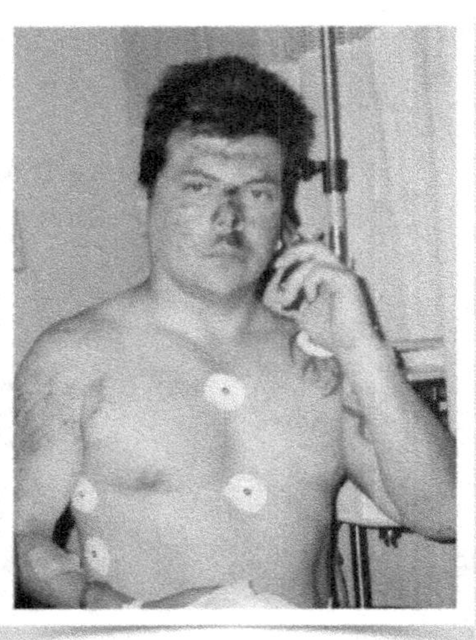

MIKE GOUCHIE
Bad Boys & Angels

Belting out a Shattered Glass tune

Big Valley Jamboree Songwriter's Tent

Mike signing CDs with Nancy Jones looking on

Bob Funk

Joel Stewart and Mike Gouchie

Kevin Churko laying down the law, and Mike Gouchie during the recording of Shattered Glass

Train Whistle
Mike Gouchie

Chapter 9

Bad Boys and Angels

First full length album done. Really, it's great for an unknown independent artist. Contrary to what some people may believe, not every recording that comes out of

Nashville, is a hit record.

Still new to these next level expectations, realizations are setting in. Maybe I am, still somewhat naive.

Another lesson learned:

"If you're not in the heart of Nashville, there's far less than a handful of people in Canada, that can help get you to that next level."

Be aware of false prophets (profits), cause they can and will eat you alive. And, often... with good intentions.

I had some very sweet people doing their best to try and help me out from time to time, trying to steer me in the right direction.

But at some point, in order to hit another plateau, you have to step up your game. If you plan on reaching any higher level of *success* without financial backing... that's one steep slope.

There still remains a lot of people out there who mean the world to me.

The one who truly helped, realized she only held so many cards. When the time came, she helped in so many ways and far beyond my expectations.

In order to *not* get totally wasted by the industry, you gotta make yourself relevant enough to shake hands with *all* the movers and shakers. And after a while, you find out there's actually not a whole lot of hands to shake...

So again, I'm being warned to steer clear of false prophets, faking their way through with good intentions.

Anyone can read a book and tell you what they think they know -- for a not so small fee.

There's nearly 3/4 of a million people in Nashville, and not all of them are big time country moguls.

So as a new artist, don't get caught up in all the Nashville hype.

When you do your homework. Do all your homework. Not all the best producers, players and singers only come out of Nashville.

It's an amazing destination, where you can learn so much and see so many cool things from the past.

It seems with today's new technology, a new artist stands a better chance of making themselves known, through social media. It's crazy right?

In my opinion, as an unknown artist with limited funding, that's the new way of getting yourself out there and noticed. Once you become relevant to millions online, the big dawgs will definitely come a calling, and you can tell them to fuck off. Kidding/not kidding, but you can make yourself a much better deal and plan moving forward because, now that you have the audience, you won't likely need to sell your soul.

I don't know for sure, maybe I'm just saying shit. Guess I sound a bit jaded, but I've learned from my own mistakes. I had outgrown the beginner stage of management and I needed to get noticed by top industry personnel. I was still wandering classrooms in the school of hard knocks. I was the one at the wheel, trying to steer myself in the "right" directions?

Success doesn't happen all on its own. And, with time you find out there's a whole lot of hoops to jump through. I was continuing to find out what that meant.

You gotta have deep pockets, or someone you know's gotta have deep pockets, and an unwavering belief in their investment.

Now, in order to reach any upper next level of success, the people who control the genre of music you're in, *they* need to know who you are, and no matter what anyone tells you, that means moola and lots of it. Any one of those controllers wanna call me out, I'll tell it straight to their face.

Here's what came directly from one of those guru's mouths, to my ears, "If you put $50 - $100K in my hands, we'll do the hard work and take care of you".

He genuinely wanted to help out and believed in my talent, but he was absolutely right. I was learning more and more how a God given gift or talent doesn't get you there on its own.

You need a full team of those who know how to get it done. That means costs, and lots of them:

As much as I appreciated his honesty and straight forwardness, the next thing he said put me off -- g*o to your Indians and they'll give you the money we need*. Man, if only it were that easy.

Hey, where's my peeps at? Maybe I'm still young enough to make another go at it... Bahahaha.

Whether it be recording music, attending a conference, paying for a flight/hotel and meals. For me, it *always* came down to, *whoever has the most money wins*. That's just *my* cold hard truth, based on *my* own personal experiences.

I was super fortunate to win a couple lotteries along the way (grants, sponsors, and loans), but never the *big* one.

Although thinking I was ready, as an independent artist, I still had no label, no big-name-management, publicist, or booking agents.

 I'd get the odd, *I'll help you out until you get paid* every once in a while, but that came with problems, so I learned to stay clear of those offers.

I just kept plugging away, keeping my head above water and providing for my family, the best way I knew how.

The Struggle Is Still Real:

Especially staying current on radio.

Most secondary radio stations were treating me quite well and kept spinning my tunes as they were being released.

But, releasing a song to radio means getting the single there through a digital media company, then hiring a radio tracker. The amount of airplay you received obviously depends on the strength of the song, but without a well-known radio tracker, your chance at large mainstream (reporting stations) radio airplay was a long shot, especially without the social media we have today.

If you're not represented by a known label, a tracker usually determines your worth to radio. The more money you have to spend on a *reputable* tracker the more likely they'll push harder to get you the spins you need (if you're relevant and have a good product). They work super hard, so it comes with a price. Most singles I released did okay, and received pretty good rotation across Canada (oddly enough, especially back east? Guess that's where they have the best taste in music.)

Was always a thrill to be driving around and hear one of my songs come on the radio. Hell of a rush.

I also released "Bad Boys and Angels" through a U.S. company that distributed the CD to radio stations around the world. It received rave reviews topping international charts weekly, over a period of several months...

Reviews coming in from New Zealand, Australia, Japan, Sweden, England, Switzerland. Stations from all around the world, including tons of secondary US stations.

Unfortunately, I didn't have the means to tour or go anywhere abroad.

Time to fill out more paperwork so "Bad Boys and Angels" can be eligible to receive accolades.

That always came with the stress of scraping up enough extra money on the side to pay the yearly memberships and entrance fees, to meet eligibility requirements...

It's not a ton for some, but it was at the time, quite a sacrifice for me.

That's right, you can have a great product, but if you don't belong to all these music industry associations and pay your yearly dues, you *do not* meet the eligibility requirements and all your hard work will go unnoticed by the awards committees.

Know your importance and always try to find a way.

Cause I mean come on, that's the only way anyone *important* is ever going to hear you.

"Bad Boys and Angels" wins the CAMA's 2006 Best Country Album and keeps the dream alive.

It's also up for a nomination at the 2006 Nammy's, in Hollywood, Florida. Once again, I find a way and fly out literally on a wing and a prayer.

I'm included as a guest on a couple documentary TV shows on APTN, with "The Mix" and "Beyond Words" which creates fantastic performance opportunities.

Local News and Media were always keeping up back home. Several more featured magazine articles follow, helping to create more forward momentum. It also piques more music industry (not always the right kind) interest.

Signed a record deal:

"Bad Boys and Angels" was now available to a worldwide market. Hopes are always that a label deal will be a game changer?

Truth for me was this label just wasn't capable of changing much. It didn't come along with management, a publicist, bookings and tracking. They just sold CD's for a profit. Turns out, even though I have a record deal and the album is being sold and distributed worldwide... 50% of 0% = 0%... Another lesson learned.

So, now I continue doing everything independently. Booking myself, paying players and paying bills.

All the record deal meant was, they could sell my CD's through their label and distribution outlets and keep the profits. Whether that was $5.00 or $500,000 who knows? (Written with a chuckle.) So, the record deal is a flop.

Whether I performed as a two piece or full band, they were always paid very well (you get what you pay for).

A performance would usually run 30-45 minute and I'd cover the players with $500 plus flights, accommodations and sometimes meals (depending on the gig or venue).

However, I always wanted to get to the point where I could have a band of my own. Everyone was a gun for hire.

One usually hires players they need, by sending charts and a setlist and hope for a rehearsal. They show up to the show, place the setlist and charts on a music stand in front of them, and do their job. If you hire the right players, you get amazing results.

I always had great players but coming from a background of running around stages and having fun with the band, made this process a bit stale and unrewarding.

I'd rather have guys who'd enjoy playing alongside me, rather than behind me. That's a lot easier said than done, cause you need to be working steady to make that happen.

I was working on it. Again, starting to fill up the calendar. Where am I gunna find some young guys and help develop them into a great live performance band?

After doing some brain storming, I stopped in at Grant McEwan University and read a note on their bulletin board.

There was a guitar or band for hire type posting. I took down the number, headed home, gathered my thoughts and made the call.

The fella who posted the add answered the phone and we hit it off right away. Soon after our conversation, he got to work and put together the rest of the band, who'd all recently graduated from music school together.

Everyone came to my house and we practiced in the basement (paid rehearsals), for our first live engagement.

I still remember them being such a great group of young musically educated guys, hungry to get out and play.

It was a Friday or Saturday night at the beer garden stage at Big Valley Jamboree. The rain is coming down heavy, at times pouring sideways into the bandshell.

Thousands kicking up mud and tilting back beverages. We powered through the weather, not skipping a beat. We made the best of the situation and had a great show.

As far as I knew, these young fellas hadn't played any big live events or shows. They were the new kids on the block, and after the show, several artists and players were asking me, "Who's your band?"

They made a great impression on me, and I had a band playing *with* me. Things were going in the right direction…

But, it's the music *Business*, sometimes things don't always go off the way you plan.

At times, it comes with a snag or two of bad luck, and *shit happens.*

An event gets cancelled and I scramble to find an alternative. This alternative turns out to be a bit of a shit show that finds me bringing my teen/preteen kids along to collect a payment. We drive into the festival and pull up beside the stage.

I tell them, "Kids stay in the van. I'll only be a few minutes". Turned on some tunes and locked up (with the windows cracked haha).

I step into the smoke-filled event trailer, closed the door and tell the buyer, *I'm not leaving until I get paid.* It had to be done and sometimes became part of the process.

Even with contracts in place, it wasn't always that simple. Trusting someone, or taking their word, set me back more than a few steps.

Another gig coming up for the full band. We're all flying out to Vancouver to do a well-paid corporate event. I had confirmations and things planned out, weeks in advance.

Morning comes. I have all the guys waiting on flight directions. Last minute the gig is cancelled, and there's nothing to recover.

I do my best to cover what I can, but the hole it created was just too deep.

And, that there my friends, is how simple and easy it can be for an independent artist, to fall to circumstances and possibly never recover, or fight even harder to make their way back up?

Still so many hidden truths to overcome.

I guess this is where the *Fake it Til You Make it* era begins.

Everyone else I knew at that time (in my age bracket) are buying homes, new vehicles and going on family vacations.

I'd been working extremely hard, trying to accomplish the same. But now, under much tighter and tougher circumstances.

Chapter 10

Rest In Peace Pops

Somewhat unexpectedly my father passes away.

He had been struggling with throat cancer over the past five years.

I'm aware of the surgery and had plans for the family to visit him during recovery. My sister calls and say, *come now*.

I drive through the night and get to the hospital. Ma hasn't left his side and immediate family is gathered in his room, around his hospital bed.

Pops, with tubes running every direction, writes me a note asking for Ma and I to go get him a cold slushy to soothe his throat. When we return a few minutes later, he is gone.

I think he knew and steered me away with Ma, so she didn't have to go through that moment when he passed.

I stayed with Ma while final arrangements were being made.

It was beautiful, as he was well loved and fondly remembered by family and countless friends.

After a beautiful eulogy, my brother, sister, and I each sang one last song for Pops... Being overwhelmed with so many emotions, thoughts and conversations, a decision

ultimately needs to be made. Go back to Edmonton, or move back to Prince George?

I line up a property caretaker position with a community housing manager to stay close to my Ma.

My engagement has become rocky throughout a year of *Fake It Til You Make it* hardships. So, at this point we go our separate ways…

Three of the kids and I stayed behind in Prince George with G Ma after dads passings. The ex fiancé and our daughter head back to their lives in Edmonton.

The new caretaker job includes a home for the kids and I to make another fresh start. Two go to their moms to finish off the school year. My oldest boy (by 20 minutes) stays with G Ma, while I head back to Edmonton, finish up a couple weeks work, then bring back our things.

It was the beginning of March and very cold outside when I got back to Edmonton and walk into a somewhat empty house, which feels even colder.

I'm finishing up work at the River Cree Resort and Casino at the time, and I managed to find a couple coworkers to come by and help load up the rest of my things.

Whatever didn't fit in the truck and trailer, I gave the guys for helping out, along with a few bucks.

It's been a long day's travel, with lots of time to reflect.

As I pull up to the new house in Prince George, with our belongings in tow, there's a yellow truck in the driveway?

I knock… Someone I know answers the door and tells me they live there now (moved in the day prior). My stomach drops to the ground and I'm left speechless.

When I gather my thoughts, I tell him my situation and the arrangements that had been made with the housing manager regarding the house and the job I'm to start.

He informs me he's made the same plans, but with someone higher up in the government.

After a quick chat, he was super accommodating and told me the home he'd just moved from down the road was available.

So, I backed out the trailer and dragged it a little further down the road to a small two bedroom trailer.

Honestly, I was heartbroken and disappointed, but super grateful we weren't left homeless. Time to make the best of it. Soon, I was unpacking, setting the place up and making the best of it.

There's plenty of room for my son and I who'd stayed behind with his G Ma. His brother and sister will be coming back after summer, to start the next school year. So, I've got time to get a bigger place...

Then a phone call comes in, which just might turn up the volume?

Chapter 11

CMT: Plucked

CMT (Country Music Television) comes a calling.

First Version:

CMT would like to invite you to take part in a new series we're putting together. We're going to choose 6 new up and coming Artists and introduce them to our Canadian Country Music Television audience. *There'll be a short documentary of your musical journey to this point, including a music video.*

This is a no brainer and meant, *a couple decades of hard work, could possibly turn into an overnight success story.*

A production crew shows up out at my Ma's family home on the Lheidli T'enneh Indian reservation, just east of Prince George. The crew chats with Ma. Then we tour around the city of Prince George, for a couple days, visiting different locations, while gathering content to fill up the documentary. The crew was sincere, amazing and everything went great.

Next: the program includes a music video.

So, the next step was choosing the right song from the current "Bad Boys and Angels album?

I remember it being somewhat of a struggle. *Do I show the softer side, or tougher side.*

Would it be, "Troublemaker, Somethin' Bout a Bad Boy or Angels Unaware?"

The softer side prevailed... CCMA Award winning video producer Joel Stewart leads the way with a story board and direction for the video.

Mike Gouchie, the story and video were amazing.

Every single thing about this first version is absolutely true. It turned out fantastic and was an incredible experience.

"My" 2nd Version:

Out of nowhere, all of a sudden this amazing opportunity turns into a contest.

All 6 Artists (groups) are now competing for a first place finish, for... *I think another video and stuff.*

I remember thinking, this just doesn't feel right.

They chose us, we didn't choose them. After all, the show's called *Plucked.*

It was misleading. So, I thought if you're going to change the narrative, you should change the name as well.

Simple, just replace the P and L with an F..."

Likely for the sake of ratings, someone came up with a bright idea. Now instead of having six winners, helping their careers, they flip it to 5 losers?

I don't know, maybe I shouldn't mention it. Cause it could come off as somewhat ungrateful, but that's not the intention...

It's like someone working super hard at a corporate job. They put in all their time and tons of effort, then the boss calls and says, *I'm giving you a promotion.* YAY.

Then, they go into work the next day and everyone's congratulating them and out of nowhere the boss says, *haha just kidding.*

Point being: It just goes to show how subjective and manipulative a competitive industry can be. Whether it's knowingly or unknowingly.

Whether it's an artist themselves (or someone who represents them), who makes one stupid little decision, it can fold you up in that super expensive suit, with you still in it.

We've all had experiences and know a person, who's made that one stupid decision that jeopardized everything. For many, it's even ourselves.

There's often *another side* of a story that goes untold. So, keep in mind. This doesn't include a single word from any other artist involved in that Series, only mine.

I wasn't a young artist with stars in my eyes; I'd been in and out of the mix for a couple decades now.

Back in Toronto in the live studio for this season finale. I'm talking to the other artists asking, *Let's try to steer this in a different direction.*

Instead of a contest, how about supporting a cross country tour including all the artists. After all, wouldn't that fall a little more in line with what we all signed up for.

I was stuck. Something "anything" other than another contest.

Too late. Once the production staff entered the room and started handing around papers, everyone (including myself) signed our lives away.

Before we know it, the finale live voting was over and someone was crowned a winner.

Or, something like that?

It may have gone down differently, but that's what I recall...

Backtrack: At the end of filming my doc, I mentioned to one of the producers "No negativity, no drama? This is great."

She says, *oh you want some drama* and of course added it. I made a comment, "I won't pay to play". And, I still stand by that statement.

I mean sure, there were and are contests like Nashville Star, Canadian/American Idol and The Voice.

But they're contests, and, you signed up for them.

You go to try-outs and auditions, knowing full well the circumstances you're getting yourself into.

But, *Any publicity is good publicity*. Right?

After the "*contest*" I get home back to BC and get message, after message, after message, from kind folks, friends and family saying they tried to vote for me, but the voting wasn't available in BC.

As victimized and jaded as this 2nd version may seem, I took the last place loss gracefully and moved on.

Like most things in life, second versions usually come with awkward truths. And, most aren't brave enough to tell them.

My story needed some drama anyways, so why not...

And, I've always been a fan of Paul Harvey's, "The Rest of the Story"

Back home things are good. I've had a couple more TV appearances on APTN's "The Mix" and "Beyond Words". More performance dates are penciled in with several more shows throughout the summer.

The school year has just ended, so my boy Skyler and I drive down to his mom's, where he'll hang with his twin brother Levi and sister Caitlyn for the summer.

Plan now is to finish up the summer schedule, then go back and pick them all up for the new school year.

Had a short vacation with the kids and headed back to Prince George. I get about 30 Km's from home, and boom...

Chapter 12

A Fork in the Road

A massive bull moose jumps out of a deep ditch onto the minivan, bending the steering wheel in half and tearing off the roof.

My passenger was fortunate to walk away without serious injury. (A prior moose incident when I was younger, took my best friend)

Unconscious from the accident, I wake up a day later in a hospital bed. My head is a mess and feeling scrambled. Guess they've run some tests and may keep me for another day or two?

Confused and blurred, I'm trying to figure out what's going on, but I'm stuttering badly and can't think or speak very well?

I have cuts and lacerations all over my face and arms. The back of my head had been opened up from ear to ear. Broken bones on one side. Thinking they'll keep me around until I was stable enough to be released, after a few more X-rays and tests.

My memory is cloudy about the situation, but I guess they released me on my own. Ma says she came to visit me, but I was no longer a patient. She found me a while later, wandering around outside in the hospital parking lot...

I had Ma drop me off at my place and refused to let anyone take care of me. She'd call several times a day to check on me and brought by food.

After a couple weeks of trying to straighten out my head, Ma picks me up and takes me to the family doctor for a follow up.

First, it turns out they put a cast on the wrong wrist and arm, so he cuts it off and puts one on the other side. Second, informs me that some tests were in and that I'll required a lot more follow up. Turns out I suffered a traumatic brain injury. *Obviously, music was on hold.*

After getting the cast off my wrist, there's a harsh realization that I've forgotten how to play guitar. And, I don't know the words to any songs I've recorded. I was recovering home alone. But Ma was always calling, to make sure I was okay. More scans and tests, followed by several months of neurotherapy and speech therapy.

After a couple months of recovery, I made the trip back down to pick up the kids. I think I rented a car, to go pick them up. When I got down to the kids I was gifted an older mid size SUV from a dear elder (like family) who would randomly help me out from time to time. So, we loaded it up and headed back home.

Chapter 13

Just Be Okay

Driving through the Rocky Mountains up on the Coquihalla Hwy. when smoke starts coming from under the hood. I realize again, what am I doing?

Tears are streaming down my face, with the hood up in the air, thinking it's a good thing the kids can't see me...

After letting the engine cool down for a while and topping off with water, we make our way back to Prince George.

We're all now living in the small trailer together. The boys in one room with bunks, daughter in the other and me on the couch.

By this time most of my friendships and relationships had fallen. My musical abilities have declined. I've hidden the frustrations and lack of strength from my kids and family. Cause, the main thing now is to recover and support my kids to get through school.

Another doctor's visit and he says, *I think you need to prepare for the worst..* This meant finding alternate care for my kids and applying for a disability pension.

None of it seemed right to me.

The following morning after breakfast, the kids walk to the school bus and head out for the day.

Alone in privacy, I break down and fall to my knees. I'm not allowed to show weakness, I can't let my kids see me declining. They didn't know it, but I needed them more than they needed me.

I prayed to whoever's out there, crying for help.

Tears pouring down like a tiny little baby needing some comfort. Begging for direction, *please* give me a sign...

A short while later I receive a phone call from the post office, just a short drive from the trailer. *There's a parcel here for you to pick up.* So, I head over to the post office store (Eastway Esso) and pick up the parcel.

I have a suspicion of what the parcel is, cause I've seen them before, but I don't know for sure, or who it's from.

Placing the parcel on the passenger seat, I turn on the vehicle. Honestly, I don't recall turning the radio on, on the ride over. The car starts and I recognize the song on the radio. "It's me."

I pull into the trailer as the song ends and grab the box. Inside I open the box and it's filled with Cd's. My CD's... I still don't know where they came from?

Taken aback, I remove my guitar from it's case by the living room couch (my bed) and put it on my lap. I close my eyes and start to play.

I can play again. I'd never been a strong guitar player and had always strummed with a pick, but somehow, my fingers on my strumming hand start to move individually plucking different strings, while my other hand makes chords. I still had a bad stutter, but as I start to sing my voice is pure.

I couldn't remember any of my own songs, but old classic songs started to come back to me.

Chapter 14

Synchronicity

My Inner Music is bringing new life.

Still in speech therapy and neuro rehab, but I can sing without stuttering. I go back to the story of Mel Tillis. He developed stuttering after a childhood illness and went on to become a country music pioneer.

It worked for Mel, so maybe I can come back from this as well.

With this stubborn brain injury comes a crazy new ability. Now I've developed a new way of thinking. And for me, now it's the right way of thinking. Mike listen to that inside voice of yours, its the one that has always stayed true.

I don't understand what it means when the doctor tells me again, that's just the way the brain works and you're going to have to learn to live with this disability.

In my mind, although I couldn't speak my thoughts clearly, I somehow knew he was wrong. I never gave up and kept teaching myself things.

Sure I've overcome obstacles in the past, but this one's different. If I'm not able to speak properly again, at least I'll be able to sing.

I'm starting to sing again. I still don't recall my own songs, so I come up with a new idea.

"If I'm going to make a new record, it's going to be the best record in the world."

I've had every other quality of record, all receiving accolades from good to better. But this, this is going to be next level. But how, how am I going to make another record and who would I get to do it?

Well, that's the easy part cause when you're brain damaged you don't know that you can't.

No one needs to know my crazy idea. I'm just going to do it, cause I believe I can. I don't have any cash, but I've done it before right, and my mind is made up and I'm going to do this.

A name keeps coming to me over and over again. It's someone I've known and admired, since the first time I started playing in a band.

Every band wanted to be like and play as well as, "The Underground Outlaws." Whether it was his family band or just Kevin, I always had a thread drawing me towards both him and his brothers' musical careers.

Now in order to get this persons attention, I'll have to send him an email. But, how embarrassing. Cause, I can't even write an email. My brain is still scrambled and I can't put together a sentence.

So, with a dictionary by my side, I spend hour after hour writing this email. I had to look up anything with four letters or more, to make sure it was spelled correctly, and I was using it properly. This was an important email, and I had to make absolutely sure that it made sense, if I was to expect a response.

I think it took me 8 - 12 hours that day, just to write a paragraph or two. After going over the email a thousand times, making absolutely sure I wasn't saying anything stupid... something told me, "just push send."

There were still a lot of things I remembered. I just had to do it, and it would come back to me.

The horned voice on one shoulder was sarcastically spewing negativity, yeah don't expect a response any time soon (if at all.) but, the Inner Music spoke with love and kindness saying, you got this.

Just a few minutes goes by and I get a response, "Hey Mike, nice to hear from you. How's it going?"

It took me a while to respond, but I get back to him asking if he'd be interested in making a record with me.

He remembered me from back in the day and asked me to send him some music. Kevin does a bit of homework on me and comes back with, I'm not really doing anything country these days, but yes I'm interested.

****

Keep in mind:

I'm still recovering from a traumatic brain injury. I can't speak with clarity and still stuttering.

Emails are my only means of communication, without provoking negative thoughts. I have no $.

I have a dream.

I'm engaging with one of my heroes.

*Kevin Churko put together a cost list and sent it out to me. I probably said, "okay I'll work on that and get back to you?"

This is BIG, now I have something to shoot for and this fresh new spark ignites a massive inferno inside.

With the dictionary still by my side, I start putting together a sponsorship package. All my past accomplishments and awards, and now a record producer with an undeniable clients list.

I didn't know anyone with deep pockets, and any past sponsorships were long dried up.

If I'm making this world class record, that's gunna require another miraculous intervention.

I'm regaining my confidence and starting to feel stronger, with speaking to people in public. The stuttering is still there, but getting better.

My entire life I've been what I guess what one calls a loner. Always going out on my own. Whether knowing someone once I got there, or just stayed to myself, it was just the norm (even today).

Out one evening, I run into an old boss and his wife. We hadn't seen each other in many years and had a great time reminiscing.

Joked about telling people they knew me, and asked if it was okay, when they told people I was their friend. Mentioning seeing me on TV and listening to me on the radio. I was reminded about a lot of things I had forgotten...

When they asked about what I was up to these days, I told them about the sponsorship I was working on and tell them about my plan for a new album, and how tough it was. Then, it turned sober serious for a moment. They told me, "We just recently won a lottery and have been looking for a good way to pay it forward". So, I met up with him the next day and passed off a sponsorship package.

They call me shortly after and want to meet up. We have some dinner and drinks and continue our chat... He reminded me of something going way way back, when we worked together.

Says, "Remember the time you lent me your camper van, so we could go on a family camping vacation?"

"I had totally forgotten, but they hadn't..."

That old camper van I used for family transportation and to haul building materials around at work, would turn out to be a true act or karma.

It certainly wasn't anything fancy, but at that moment, it as my golden chariot. "Mike, we've come to a decision and would like to help with sponsoring your new album".

Part of the sponsorship package I managed to put together, included putting all the funds through a music foundation, I'd previously worked with, which allowed the sponsor to receive a 100% tax receipt from the non-profit music foundation.

A cashiers check was written out for the total amount Kevin had projected for the album. I let Kevin know we're ready to go, and the ball starts rolling.

Everything is set. I go meet up with my new co-producer Bob Funk in Nashville and set up more writing sessions.

Kevin puts full trust in Bob and says, "he's my Nashville guy". I follow his lead and am not disappointed in any way. Bob's a beautiful human being and never settles for anything less than perfect. I ended up writing one of my favorite songs with his wife Patricia.

I'm still not speaking very well, but my speech is improving daily. However, *it does create an incident in Nashville, I no longer speak of.*

Recording the album:

Now this process is more than anything I'd experienced in the past. I was given respect. And, anything I wanted, or suggested was taken 100% seriously. I was making some real true friends in the top end of the music-world.

Off to Sound Stage Studios and Apartment Studio in Nashville where we lay down some tracks.

On the way home from Nashville, a past manager and my favorite musical friend of all time Maryanne Gibson, happened to be on the same flight. We chat for a while, and I get caught up with what's going on, then she hands me a book by George Jones "I Lived to Tell It All".

She tells me she has just finished reading it and she'd like me to have it.

I brought the book back home and spent night after night reading (and crying) until it was complete.

I recall thinking, *one day I'd like to shake this man's hand.*

I'd brought Mom and Dad to a George Jones and Tammy Wynette concert a few years earlier in Prince George. That concert created a forever memory, and of course, George was one of dad's favorites.

Bob had the album done up to the point, where I could head out to Vegas and record final vocal tracks with Kevin.Sitting on the airplane to Las Vegas, I'm on the aisle seat. The lady in the middle seat seems uncomfortable. I smile at her, but she doesn't say much. I had red streaks in my hair, a headband, no sleeves and tattoos. Guess I didn't look very approachable...

At some point she had to go to the washroom, so she asked me if I could let her sneak past. I stood up so she could pass, and when she came back we started a conversation.

She explained that she'd thought I was a famous actor or something, and she expected that I wouldn't want to be disturbed. I had a good laugh about that.

She was dressed up in some nice country duds, and was off to the PBR (Professional Bull Riding) Finals.

I told her I was off to record vocals for my new country album. She asked, "do you have any music with you?"

I had a CD of Bad Boys and Angels in my carry on, so I reached above the seat into the luggage compartment and grabbed a copy. She took the CD which had my phone number and contact information on it, and when the plane landed said goodbye and we wished each other well.

The Wolfe's Lair in Las Vegas NV.

I think Kevin had the vocals penciled in for four days?

I'd never been coached or told any certain way for singing vocals. But, Kevin brought out the best in my voice. I figured it was because he had a stick to smack me with if I didn't get it right – or so I insinuated..

We learned a lot about each other over the next few days. Real people sharing real experiences.

He'd just bought a new home and was kind enough to put me up in his old house/studio (The Wolfe's Lair), while I was there recording. I had such a great time being treated like I belonged. He'll probably never know it, but I consider him one of the best friends I've ever had (for reasons you'll learn later). I still follow what he's up to these days, but we haven't seen each other in about 15 years.

We finished up all the vocals a day early, so Kevin treated me to a night out. Each with a tray full of poker chips, we played poker for the night, at a local Vegas casino and had some more laughs and just an honest good time.

Another unfortunate turn of events:

The Canadian dollar was better than the American dollar at the time (believe it or not), and when the Canadian dollar crashed it left the music foundation short on payment. "Kevin was much cooler with this situation than I had experienced with the previous album."

He said to me, "I've been quite blessed with my career Mike, and where things are going. I'm fine with the payment up to date, just make sure you take care of Bob" And, I gave him my word.

When Kevin dropped me off at the airport (a week before Christmas), his handshake filled mine with a very unexpected gift. He said, "I hope you and your kids have a beautiful Christmas" followed by a quick man hug.

For him, it may have been a simple kind gesture, but for me, it spoke straight to my heart. I went home and enjoyed Christmas with my family.

Over the next while Bob and Kevin and his son Kane worked on completing the album. When it was finished it was everything I had hoped for and more.

Without a doubt I don't believe there's anyone who worked on or pre-viewed that record, who would say it wasn't a world class record.

I couldn't wait to have it pressed and start shopping it around.

There was a quiet buzz, but a buzz just the same. *I was making yet another comeback, but this time I had the record to back it up.*

In the meantime, I'm experiencing some throat issues that keep popping up...

My doctor sends me to a throat specialist in Vancouver, as a precautionary measure, since my father died of throat cancer.

I go to the appointment and the scare is averted with good news. It is just overuse and some straining issues, and once I rest my vocal cords I should recover completely.

Walking back to my hotel room, I receive a phone call. I'm standing on West Broadway when a lady's voice in my ear says, *hey is this Mike*? I respond *yes*.

She says, "I met you on an airplane to Vegas a few months back". I say, "Of course I remember you"...

I had absolutely no idea why she was calling and at the time, I don't know if she knew either?

She asks where I am, and I tell her Vancouver. She says, "whereabouts?" I tell her "West Broadway, and I'm just heading across the street to Earl's for some lunch".

She says, "No way. I'm a block away. Do you mind if I join you?" "I have no idea where this is going?"

I'm sitting in Earl's for going on 20 minutes, and becoming a bit puzzled, when she finally walks in and says, "Hey sorry, I have a big truck and its tough to find parking, then I was on the phone for awhile." I stand up, and she joins me at the table.

"After I parked," she continues, "I called another gentleman I met on a flight to Florida about a year ago. I told him about you, and he'd like to meet. It's all just too coincidental, calling you, you being here and his office being just down this street".

Serendipity.

After lunch she drives me down the road to his office, and as we're walking up the stairs, I notice photos of some of the biggest touring artists and bands from around the world.

In his office introductions are made around a large table. His dog Hank comes over and makes friends.

After an hour or so of getting to know each other, he asks me a question that blows my mind..

"How do you think you'd go over opening for George Jones, on a cross Canada tour?" *Wow*. I tell him "I'm a big fan and grew up on his music, I would love the opportunity". "Okay," he says, "let me look into a few things and I'll get back to you in a couple weeks".

This all happened within a matter of hours:

I walk out of a throat cancer scare, and someone I met on an airplane to Vegas randomly calls. She asks to join me for lunch, and then she introduces me to a touring manager, and suddenly I'm potentially on a tour with George *Freakin'* Jones..

I get back home and don't say a word to anyone. I do some research, and my guy's as legitimate as they get.

It's only a few days later when the call comes in, and he says, "Let's make it official. You're the opening act for George Jones on a cross Canada tour."

I go out to my Mom's and tell her the great news, that I've signed a management deal and am opening for George Jones on his 2009 North American Tour.

Ma is thrilled and says come with me my boy. She walks into her room and opens one of the closet doors, where she pulls out a guitar case that she's tucked away for the past couple years. She lays it on the bed and opens the case. It's my dad's pride and joy, his holy grail. He always said, "before I go I want to own the best sounding guitar ever". And there it is, his 2003 *Larrivée.*

Ma says, "Mike I know your dad's proud of you, and I think you should take him with you on your tour with George Jones".

With and without the guitar, I'd always felt the presence of my Pops every step of the way.

I prepared for the tour like a well-trained athlete. I ran with my dog Diesel 5 to 10 kilometers a day, with my headphones in listening to my songs over and over.

I made sure every note, and every voice movement, was meticulously mastered so I'd be at my absolute best.

One day while on a run with Diesel, my manager called and goes off on me. Apparently one of the guys coming on tour with me made the mistake of calling and asking my manager if he'd be interested in selling him the lower mainland date.

My manager called me and lost his shit, cussing like a sailor and said, *if you wanna keep this tour, you'd better call him and tell him he can F*** right off.*

I made the call and had to let him know we were finding someone else for the tour.

It turned out for the best, with new accompaniments Linda Kidder on bass and back up vocals, and the great Brent Shindell on guitar. Linda and Brent brought so much experience and professionalism with them, they were amazing.

Linda sang and toured with KD Lang, and in another full circle moment, she won best group or duo with the fella I fell third place to in my first talent contest-- Gary Fjellgaard. Brent was best known to me for his time playing with Doucette.

It was surreal when in Vancouver for rehearsals at Brent's house. There it is, his Juno for Doucette's "Mama Let Him Play".

Time to fly:

October 4 to October 25, 2009, we fly out of Vancouver to Winnipeg, to meet up with the George Jones tour. They were coming up from the first half of their U.S. tour.

Once we landed we headed to the hotel, where we met the tour planner Barb, who showed us to our tour bus. This would be our home for all the weeks of the tour. The next morning we went to the arena, met George Jones' long time stage manager and drummer, by the name of Bobby. He gave me my All Access Pass and attached it to his personal Heisman Trophy lanyard. From the get-go George Jones' stable treated us great.

Starting with the sound check right up through to standing on that first stage, the experience was everything I had ever dreamed about. Just imagine, standing on the stage waiting to open for the Legendary, one and only George Jones. I can still close my eyes and relive that feeling any time I choose, and I'll be doing that for the rest of my days...

First Night:

The set is going amazing. Brent and Linda exit the stage, and I do one acoustic song on my own.

With permission, I use George's stool and play a Vince Gill cover "Sight for Sore Eyes".

After everything I'd gone through to get to this point, this song spoke to me.

When I ask Linda and Brent to come back out and do a feature of their own, in the darkness backstage, Linda stumbles and falls to the ground.

There's a loud thud, but she gets up and there she is playing her bass with one hand. Brent is playing his guitar. Linda is bleeding since when she fell, she hit her face on the drum riser, but she keeps on playing without missing a note.

She insists we keep playing and finish up the rest of the songs! Then, and only then, she lets them shuttle her off to emergency where she gets stitched up.

Without a doubt in my mind, if it were any other human being, they would've exited stage without conversation and headed straight to the hospital.

The first night at the end of the show I was approached by a staffer and asked if I'd like to join George for his last song of the night. I imagine my response was unexpected, but I knew it was right.

"I'd love to," I said, "but it's the first show and I just haven't earned it yet." "Okay," he replies, "you let us know when you're ready and we'll make it happen."

* * *

My oldest daughter, Caitlyn, joined us for the tour to help out with merchandise.

Nancy Jones took Caitlyn under her wing and showed her the ropes.

One night Nancy told me she loved old classic rock, so we learned Credence Clearwater Revivals Cotton Fields and played a dedication to her.

Most concerts have a small section behind or beside the stage with no public access.

I found that spot several nights and would just sit there, all on my own watching and listening.

On a night early into the tour, tears of comfort started flowing, as I remembered my father sitting there with me...

The tour just kept getting better and better. We'd finish my 45 minute set, then I'd rush out to the lobby to sign CD's before the main show. This was real...

When we hit Red Deer, Alberta, there's a break for a couple days before the next show.

That's when we got a dinner invite to join George, Nancy and the Jones Boys.

A restaurant was reserved for us, that night, and we all sat around a table with George telling stories and all of us sharing pictures. He talked about his twin grandsons, and I told him about my twin boys. George's group made me feel just like one of the family. I'd recently finished his book that had been gifted to me and George was kind enough to sign it for me.

Three shows into the tour, we hit Edmonton and my mom and brother were flown in, and my aunt and uncle from Prince George also joined them.

Being well known in Edmonton at this time, the stop turned out to be super chaotic.

Both my daughters helped out with merch sales during the break after my opening set.

After the show there was an organized meet and greet with family and friends in my dressing room attended by my mother, brother, aunt and uncle, my daughters, a past manager and a couple of music friends. It was just a small gathering but for some reason, it made for an uncomfortable discussion later on with my management. I believe the words *you're just an opening act* were used, and the end result was, there were no more "meet and greets".

Along the way, the girl I was seeing, wanted to set up a beautiful gesture with a local guitar maker. The idea was to surprise me with a personalized guitar on stage.

I guess that phone call "didn't go over very well w/ management",

but after the show the guitar maker came backstage and gifted me with a very special Prairie Custom Shop guitar. It has a photo of all my kids engraved into the back neck plate.

When Caitlyn was done with the portion of the tour she came along for, she headed back home to work. The tour carried on eastward, and as it was coming to an end, I felt it was time....

It was the last night of the tour, and I was ready to share the stage with George Jones. Linda joined me on stage and we both sang along side *The Possum,* "I Don't Need Your Rockin' Chair..."

It was well worth the wait and a true lifetime experience. Yes, I could have accompanied George every night, but this was my way of showing respect for one of the most iconic country music super stars of all time. I have no regrets.

Okay maybe one regret. I was offered the stool that had accompanied George Jones on stage for many years, but I was flying home from back east to British Columbia after the tour, and I had nowhere to put it on the plane. "I Don't Need your Rockin' Chair", but that stool would've been an amazing keepsake.

A couple of months after the tour Christmas came along and I received a package of George Jones coffee in the mail from Nancy. It's still part of my George Jones shrine, along with other amazing memories from the tour.

Linda and Brent became great friends throughout the George Jones tour, so much so that the label hired them for shows afterward. I had another near miss with Linda in Arlington Washington, where we were detained at the border--thanks to me, I'm sure. When we were finally released and got to the festival, the stage was so hot, Linda nearly burned her feet off. With that in mind, I hired them independently for cooler stages, up in Whitehorse, Yukon and other northern climates.

Further down the road, I'll record more music and hire Linda and Brent for their musical parts.

Chapter 15

My own tour?

Label/Management has been busy planning, with a couple festivals coming up, I head out on an acoustic tour visiting brain injury groups.

I Called up an old guitar playing buddy of mine and he struck a deal with my Label/Management. Along the way I'd call up radio stations and put together last minute house concerts. No cost, just let us sell CDs (we had lots), if they wanted them.

Everything was going great. We were selling lots of CD's. I was making enough to maintain our fuel, hotels, and meal costs.

Management made a deal with the guitar player (which I had no part in) for direct payment through the label.

When they were late, the guitar player (after a few drinks) let my manager know he wanted his money. Of course my manager later let me know.

Now it became my responsibility. I'm the one who brought him along, so if I wanted to keep my deal I'd need to figure it out...

Once again, it was super uncomfortable getting in the middle, while seeing both sides. We carried on and I kept them both happy, making the payments from CD sales.

The final straw was at BVJ. It was our last stop (or became the last stop) on the tour. A kind gentleman loaned me a motorhome to take to the festival. Instead of parking behind the stages like all the other artist, I thought it might be a great idea to get a space out with the fans.

First night turns out to be a bad idea. Super rowdy and no sleep whatsoever. The next day we changed spots. Still with the fans, but a mature crowd.

Let's get a couple girls to sell CDs throughout the festival weekend.

The guitar player decides it's best if his wife comes out with her friend and they'll sell CDs.

I'm not going to argue at this point, our tour is nearly over and I've already been put in an awkward position between career and friendships...

They show up and he takes all his belonging and moves over to another section with his wife and their friends. This is fine, I get the RV to myself. I go with the flow but start feeling a bit disrespected. My thoughts were, It's the label you're having issues with man, not me. Even though he was paid in full, more true colors keep popping up, induced by liquid courage.

We have a great set the next afternoon in the songwriters tent, but my CDs didn't make an appearance until the show was over. I go hang out with some of the other artists backstage.

I've set up a large poster and CD display on the front window of the RV and we have a small P/A system that hooks up to the RV and I've arranged to play a set every few hours, between main stage performances.

People have been enjoying the music and bringing chairs over and setting up. The first set or two go over great.

The ongoing issue between my guitar player and manager becomes more fueled by alcohol, and starts to affect the quality of playing, so I unplug and shut things down.

A day or two later I have a show in Halifax, minus a guitar player...

This was a first for me, because every person in the crowd seemed to be singing along to all my songs.

Next stop:

Management has developed a record label and the touring company has joined up with Ticketmaster to help promote a Mike Gouchie cross Canada tour. I believe we ended up with 22 dates or so...

I visited Ticketmaster in Toronto and was told I was the first artist to play an acoustic show for their staff?

Anyone visiting Ticketmaster online to order any ticket would see a banner of Mike Gouchie on top of the site announcing the tour and ticket sales, along with a free single download of Shattered Glass.

The first HMV music stores I walked into, I see my CD on the shelf. Wow. There's Mike Gouchie right in the middle between Merle Haggard and George Jones! Even if I'm only there by alphabetical coincidence, I'm still there.

During this big build up for the new tour, management/label is calling often with plans filled with excitement.

We're gunna plaster your face all over billboards and busses like Michael Bublé. "Mike, you have such an incredible story, we should make a movie based on your life".

I was in, hook, line and sinker... It was quite an amazing feeling to be thought of in such regard, by someone that high in the industry. I had no reason to doubt any of it...

The tour was approaching and I'm asked, "What do you want. Like seriously, what kind of money are you thinking of making and what are your expectations?"

I say, "I just want a house on the lake where my Ma can come watch my boys, while I'm out on tour. As long as we have enough to be comfortable, I'm happy..."

Response was, "Sounds reasonable, I can appreciate that." You can imagine the anticipation and excitement building.

Any earnings for performance and cd sales, went to the new label. I believe I was sent $2,000 a month for living expenses and enough to get by.

A fully furnished lake house becomes available, but this is where things get fuzzy... I'm ready to make the move and pay things forward by giving away and gifting everything in our home.

The boys and I pack up the rest of our things and we're off once again. This time with nothing more than a truck full of memories.

Arriving down south to the home we believe we're moving into, there's an old fella on the porch. He says, "my wife and I split up and that deal fell through. I'm staying here and the place isn't available anymore".

I call my Label/Management and get no response. I believe that's when/where the deal, tour and everything falls apart.

Don't know for sure what's happened? Heard a bunch of rumors, but just left it at that...

At that same time, I'd just finished up an interview with Country Music News. They're gracing me with the cover and feature story.

I'm left to my own assumptions and blaming myself for some unknown reason:

What went wrong? What did or didn't I do?

After a time and on down the road a bit, I had some time to reflect and process things, and I sent that manager an email telling him how grateful I was. Because regardless of any shortcomings, without him, I would never of had the amazing opportunities and experiences touring with George Jones!

Downside, now no other label or management would touch me or the "Shattered

Glass" album with a ten-foot pole. "It's just business..."

Chapter 16

Half A Quorum

Life lived to date has brought many hardships, but also several blessings. A single dad with no fixed income or child support, I often found myself doing whatever it took, and always found a way...

So, life lesson #4,682 "Don't play victim to life's unfortunate circumstances. Continue moving forward and make the best of every situation".

Like I said... "it was just me, the boys, and a truck full of memories".

I made some calls and found someone who allowed us to stay in her travel trailer for a while.

The boys are 15 and need to be enrolled in school, which is starting in just a few days. Feeling like a broke joke, I take a cash job the next day and start looking for a place nearby. The boys stay focused on what they want to take in school. There's only one school in the country that provides the apprenticeship program they're interested in.

I get an advance from the guy I'm working with, and it isn't long before I find a small furnished basement suite near the school and we move in.

Life goes on...

Once somewhat stable, I start burning the candle at both ends again. Working every daylight hour possible and playing private opportunities to make a little extra on the side.

There's an award show coming up in Vancouver.

A solid friend Pat (Sean) comes down and says, "we're going". Takes me out, insists on buying me a suit for the performance and drives us down to the 2010 BCCMA's in

Vancouver B.C.

The house band was great and my small part in the awards show was successful.

Being in Vancouver around other artists management and label personalities rumours start flying...

Questions being asked about my music career, the general answer becomes, "had a deal, the deal didn't work out and now I'm moving on". Hmm, that sounds familiar.

My boys and I move to another low income condo. I find an add from a real estate lady selling some of her old staging furniture.

I furnish the "entire" place for around $500, which helped us out a great deal.

The boys are now playing Varsity football. I'm proudly paying the $5 cover at Friday Night Lights, to watch them play.

They start getting into MMA and are growing into young men, so I stay close to home.

I have another award show coming up and start looking for a band. I go out one night to a local Kelowna night club. I see an old bass player from Gunshy, playing with a great band (Half a Quorum).

After their set, Terry comes over and introduces the guys.

I ask them if they'd be interested in playing some music with me.

I'm sure they do some background checks, to see if I'm legit. Then we start rehearsals and playing shows.

We play an award show in Kelowna, where I win a couple award categories, including Country/Bluegrass Recording of the Year and Aboriginal Recording of the Year for "Shattered Glass" at the 2011 BCIMA's. These become the 3rd and 4th wins for the album. After several more shows and festivals together, we hit the Merritt Mountain Music Festival.

The boys have now graduated high school and the folks I'm now renting a house from in Summerland came along to the show.

They stayed and sponsored a motel room in Merritt for the night. The other band guys all drove back home to Kelowna, Vernon and Kamloops after the show.

It's July 7th and snow and sleet is coming sideways into the bandshell. The weather was so bad for the rest of the night, we stayed in our trailer backstage and didn't even go out to see the main headliner who was one of my favourite "country" voices, Joe Nichols. But, we could hear loud and clear from inside the trailer, staying warm and dry.

We play a few more shows together. I meet a talented keyboard player through the band, and we start a relationship.

Makes financial sense to book just her and I as a duo, for the next up and coming shows.

The boys go to work on the oil rigs and I continue working and playing music when the opportunities arise.

One of my boys calls me from up north and we have a heart to heart. This is when a moment of clarity hits me like a ton of bricks.

"For the first time in 20 years, I don't have any home obligations." What's stopping me from going out and touring full time?

Nothing.

Oh, wait a minute... Yup, money.

At 17, my boys are out quadrupling their dad's monthly income.

New plan:

Now that I'm free to explore my own options, I put a feeler out on social media. "I'm looking for leads on industrial jobs in oil and gas. I get a response from one of Johnny Reid's biggest fans.

Says, "My husband works for a company in Estevan Saskatchewan and would hire you on".

I went to Okanagan University College, got all the certificates required, and headed southeast.

In Estevan, working cement and acid, I get my air brakes, Class 1 and an education on fracking.

Rigging in/out. Pumping down hole through the winter months, with half of it at -50°C.

After fulfilling a six month agreement, I'd saved enough, and I decide to go a different route. So, I head back to school.

Now that I know I can make some real money, I'm going back to what I've always loved besides music... The environment.

I go back to school and get more certificates and start work with an environmental company. Jobs are a couple months here, a couple months there... I finish up the latter and hear an add on the radio.

"We're looking for 20 B.C. residents to write a 1500 word essay and submit it to TransCanada, for Occupational Health and Safety Officer training scholarship opportunities.

I go home, immediately write an essay. The next day I get a call from the TransCanada rep saying, *we'd like to have you on board, if you're interested.*

I accept.

Still planning to play music, but this time on my own terms.

On the last day of graduation, I get a call asking if I'd be interested in a job interview".

I thought I had landed one of the TransCanada OH&S positions, and after the interview it turns out to be somewhat related, but not the job I expected at all.

Harry (the fella who interviewed me and who remains a good friend), sets me up with a new contractor position.

That next day, I start putting together my own company (Noostel: translates to Wolverine), and I start contract work almost immediately.

Music under my own terms is getting closer and closer...

In this new world as an Environmental Specialist/Inspector, I'm getting absolutely hooked on earning and investing.

There was definitely a much different look, to my new office.

I was living large from time to time but paid myself a minimum salary.

Now back in Prince George, looking to purchase the place I'm in with my boys renting the suite in the basement.

Basically home for a week, work for a month. Repeat...

Things are on track and I'm building a great new life. Savings are growing large... I'd booked a couple corporate music dates playing on my own. Then another snag:

Harry and I decide to go for a coffee and walk across from our office on 4th and Victoria when a car runs me down. I'm hooked up to a traction board and get rushed to the hospital. Priorities go back to healing and getting back to work asap.

A chance meeting with my old high school crush, finds me looking for local contracts. I land the next couple years' contracts, and our fateful meeting turns into a beautiful marriage. Together we watch our mixed family grow.

One night while playing guitar and singing "Sunshine" by Nazareth, we decide it's time for me to go record some more music.

I contact my long time pal Michael Ohman and we have a discussion about what it looks like, to work on this new project together.

Mike pretty much sets everything up, for the recording "cause that's just what he does". And, I go back to work so I can take a week off to go record...

My company continues earning great figures and I tell my wife Cheryl, *okay, just two more years and we'll retire.*

Chapter 17

Train Whistle

The new Live (ish) album "Train Whistle" 2020 is made up of 6 self penned songs and one old classic rock ballad, which inspired the album, is recorded at *Studio Downe Under* with an incredible crew. I tell the story behind each song and go through each acoustically. Once the guys grab the feel we go live. It's another great experience with new/old friends...

Train Whistle:

An industrial song featuring vocal inserts of Chief Dan George's Lament for Confederation 1967

Sunshine:

Nazareth Cover

Money Ain't Everything:

Written from the experiences of a friend. She and her son escaped a dangerous situation which left her no alternative, but to work in an unthinkable industry

Leap of Faith:

A divorce experience, with a man trying to make his way back though music

Angel:

The experience you feel towards a woman, when finding true love

Sweet Love:

Written for my daughter Mariah and son in law Shane's engagement experience and sang at their wedding.

I'd Do it Over Again:

Written about errors in life. And, making things right not only through words, but proving it with love.

While thinking about retirement, a call comes in while I'm finishing up as the Enviro Inspector on an explosion close to home.

Still in work gear, I go out to a local Prince George restaurant for the interview and landed a four year contract as a Coordinator for the largest private sector investment in Canadian history.

Music would be on hold for just a bit longer...

During this time, we both worked hard and we bought a beautiful home. After about a year we renovate it into our forever home and keep investing.

We find a cabin on a lake, that we pay for in full, and now we have a summer cabin.

After enjoying it for a couple summers it's time to start making some real retirement plans.

I make all the proper arrangements (so we thought) for cabin to come down and put up our new home. We design our new retirement place, make plans to sell our current home and make the move.

Everything is coming together, then another snag. While in the process of an archeological dig, remains are found and a stop work order is put on the build.

We agree on Plan B and end up recouping about 25% of our investment, but don't give up on the lake retirement dream.

While I'm down south dealing with the current property issues, Cheryl finds another listing. I'm standing on the current property when the real estate agent calls. I tell him

I'm about 30 minutes away and head back towards home to have a look.

Turning in, it's an area where I grew up and spent summers. It feels just right. The agent shows me the new house and I tell him *sold*.

I get back on the road and call Cheryl to tell her, *well, looks like we just bought a new lake house.* She's absolutely thrilled.

The next weekend we drive down and meet up with the real estate agent and the landowner sisters.

I tell the sisters, *I used to throw hay bales in that field (across from the new house) for my uncle, when I was a kid.*

They ask, *oh, who was your uncle?*

I tell them about my uncle and his identical twin brother.

Their response, *We knew them very well, your uncle was our stepfather.*

WOW....

Without a doubt, everything happens for a reason.

You may recall me mentioning to a manager, awhile back in the story, *all I want is a house on a lake, that my family can enjoy.*

I'd worked extremely hard in the "m"usic "B"usiness, to achieve this same goal several times.

Life lessons:

It's never too late Trust in yourself

Rely on your own instincts

It's okay to set different goals, to reach the same objectives Never give up

We bought our dream lake house. A journey finally told...

Recently, I've put together a small home studio and am ready to get back to what I love. Music with a capital "M", removing the BS from business.

The studio view encourages music to flow smoothly and also inspired me to write this book...

I'd been looking into doing a duet with someone very special... April 7, 2025, 2:30 pm. I'm sitting in my studio writing, when the phone rings, and a voice says, *hi, is this Mike,* in a Southern Nashville accent. *This is Georgette* (George Jones and Tammy Wynette's daughter). *I just wanted to call you personally and talk about your song. It's a beautiful song.* When the opportunity came to do a duet with Georgette, it just felt right for both of us to do a song I wrote titled, "I'd Do It Over Again", and it's in the works...

Writing this book I've had countless private conversations with my *inner music.*

Just tell your truths and be as kind as possible while doing so. It was easy for the most part.

After all, not every hand we're dealt with, is a winner.

If you still want a seat at the table, accept each hand you're dealt with and learn from it. And, if you play your cards right, you just may end up with the best hand after all...

The *inner music* brings the calm...

But, I still had questions. Like, *why did I fail so many damn times in life and in music,* and *why did you lead me in one direction, only to pull the rug out from underneath me towards another.*

Reflecting on all the losses and tough times... has helped me to realize, "had I not, I may never have actually earned this life I always dreamed of."

Eventually, I learned to listen to the right voice.

Depending on my state of mind and understanding of the things around me, sometimes it was easy to confuse the two.

Especially when it was something I wanted badly.

In some of my darkest days, somehow that calm powerful voice, had unknowingly kept me from falling.

For those of you still wondering about the voice in my head... Time to introduce you to my *"Inner Music"*.

When I was born there were two of us. My twin was lost at birth and when I found this out, everything -- and I mean everything -- changed and started to make sense.

I know there are skeptics and non-believers in spirituality out there. But without a doubt, I've had someone looking out for me my entire life, and, I believe we'll be together in the next lifetime as well.....

To this day we don't know if my twin died, or was taken and given to another family? That's just how things worked back then. Especially with indigenous women and families...

A calm peacefulness surrounds me now, more than ever. Knowing I'll never truly be alone.

Yesterday's discomforts, today's embraces and tomorrow's encouragement all stand alongside me -- my ancestors, my family.

I am, where I'm supposed to be...

An old friend pops up on a social media feed. She's an author, with several successful titles to her credit.

I jokingly/non jokingly ask if she'd like to write a book for me. She kindly declines having her own obligations. She tells me she's very busy, but she encourages me to write my own story.

We get reacquainted, and she happens to be involved with a publisher, so she points me in the right direction. And again, perfect timing.

I sign a publishing deal with BWL Publishing and I write this book. What's next...

A book/musical journey tour?

Good things still lie ahead. And no matter what, I'll stay the course and ride it out.

Come along on the road with me, as I try to make sense of it all:

Closing in on greatness

A washed-out trail ending in failure Deflated and stranded

Standing strong

Another light at the end of the tunnel goes black. An exciting ride gets derailed repetitively.

Things that just don't happen. Unless, you're Mike Gouchie...

Please leave
a review.

Mike Gouchie is a multi award winning Indigenous Nashville Country Recording Artist.

Over his musical career he's had the privilege of opening for Country Legend George Jones on a cross Canada tour and has shared stages with Alan Jackson, Lonestar, Billy Currington, the Neville Brothers, Jo Nichols among more...

Mike Gouchie has lived the kind of life most only sing about. A ten-time award- winning Country Recording Artist with deep Indigenous roots, Mike's journey through the highs of the spotlight and the lows of life behind the curtain is as real as it gets.

In *Shattered Glass*, he shares his raw and riveting story—an unfiltered look at the pursuit of a dream in an industry that rarely plays fair.

From standing ovations to slammed doors, from almost making it to almost giving up, this memoir is a heartfelt tribute to resilience, faith, and the power of never letting go. Along the way, Mike lets you in on the backstage moments, the near-misses, and the personal struggles that shaped the man behind the music.

Because sometimes, the ones who *almost made it* are the ones with the most powerful story to tell.

www.ingramcontent.com/pod-product-compliance
Lightning Source LLC
Chambersburg PA
CBHW080451030726
47592CB00011B/3069